CW01663689

To
My dearest friend, Renie.

Lots of love

from

Rollie

Guernsey Sentinel

The Remarkable Les Hanois Lighthouse

by Ray Dafter

Dedicated to the memory of Paul Goldsmith,
son of Robbie and friend of the Hanois Keepers,
who lost his life at sea

Matfield Books

1. An original water colour painting of Les Hanois Lighthouse by former lighthouse keeper and artist Barry Hawkins. The painting was specially commissioned for this book.

First published 2003
Published by:
Matfield Books, PO Box 289, Tonbridge, TN12 7UG, England

Copyright © Ray Dafter 2003

The right of Ray Dafter to be identified as the author of this work
has been asserted in accordance with
the Copyright, Design and Patents Act 1988

ISBN 0-9540595-1-4

All rights reserved. No part may be reproduced, stored in a retrieval system or transmitted, in any form or by any means, electronic, mechanical, photocopying, recording or otherwise without the prior written permission of the author and publisher. This book is sold subject to the condition that it shall not by way of trade or otherwise be lent, resold, hired out or otherwise circulated without the publisher's prior consent in any form of binding or cover other than that in which it is published.

A catalogue record for this book is available from the British Library

Printed and bound by Principal Colour
Hop Pocket Lane Paddock Wood Kent
TN12 6DQ England

2. A fine day at Les Hanois. (Barry Hawkins)

3. A spectacular aerial view of Les Hanois lighthouse, clearly showing the two helipads. (Brian Green)

Les Hanois Lighthouse

Contents

INTRODUCTION

Strictly speaking, a sentinel is a person – someone who stands guard or keeps watch. But at times it seems Les Hanois Lighthouse does have a life of its own. It certainly had a difficult conception. Its birth in 1862 was historic. And since then it has done much to protect both mariners and the keepers who tended the warning light.

Les Hanois is truly a remarkable lighthouse. Erected on a treacherous reef on the western point of Guernsey, the lighthouse is a beacon for vessels entering the Channel Traffic Separation Scheme. Built in response to a spate of fateful shipwrecks the lighthouse has helped to prevent numerous maritime accidents since it became operational.

It is the most southerly of the lighthouses in the UK administered by the Corporation of Trinity House. It was the first rock tower to be constructed using dovetailed granite stones integrated both horizontally and vertically. It was the first to use photovoltaic cells as an electrical power source. And it was the last Trinity House rock tower to be manned.

The lighthouse has been the scene of personal tragedy and drama. During the 1939-45 war the tower fell under German occupation. But throughout its history it has also witnessed acts of bravery, folly and humour.

Often eclipsed by the public attention afforded to the more famous lighthouses, Les Hanois has nevertheless earned the affection of all those associated with the Channel Islands. The striking tower, perched on its rocky outcrop, has been depicted in countless photographs and paintings as well as on bank notes and postage stamps.

And yet, strange as it may seem, in the early days the planned construction of the lighthouse was met with concerted opposition: by shipowners and the local Chamber of Commerce; even by Trinity House itself which not only claimed it had no jurisdiction over lighthouse construction in Guernsey but also stated that a tower on Hanois would do more harm than good or, to be precise: "would probably be productive of much greater mischief to the general trade passing up and down Channel than it could possibly prove of benefit to the local navigation of those islands".

This then is the story of Les Hanois Lighthouse, told as a result of extensive research into the archives and conversations with many of the lighthouse keepers who served in that rock tower. The story recounts the history of the lighthouse, highlights the numerous shipwrecks and maritime mishaps associated with that part of Guernsey, and features the exploits of the dedicated men who served at Les Hanois.

It is a story that could not have been written without the help of many individuals and organisations. I would particularly like to thank the staff of Guernsey Museums and Galleries; the States of Guernsey Island Archives Service; the Priaulx Library in St Peter Port; the Guernsey Shipwreck Museum at Fort Grey; Guernsey Post Office; D M Clark, Guernsey States Treasurer; Guernsey Press; the Guildhall Library in the City of London; Trinity House; the Royal Institution; the National Army Museum; the Commissioners of Irish Lights; the Lighthouse Society of Great Britain; the Association of Lighthouse Keepers and Westminster Reference Library as well as members of the Channel Islands Maritime History Group at www.smartgroups.com. All have been generous with their time and knowledge. I am also grateful to Rob Blann for the use of various excerpts from his website www.YourMemories.co.uk.

Among the many individuals who have assisted me by providing reminiscences, anecdotes and advice I would like to acknowledge in particular Ken Trethewey of the Lighthouse Society of Great Britain; Capt Robert Barton, St Peter Port Harbour Master; Howard Cooper, George Oldham, Gordon Head and Karen Potter of Trinity House; Nathan Arnold, Martin Boyle, Jack Daniels, Paul Davis, Alan Laing, Dave McGovern, Karl and Hans-Günter Spitzer, Norman Wakley and Richard Tostevin. I must give special thanks to Matt Harvey, Social History Officer of Guernsey Museum Services, Gerry Douglas-Sherwood, the Association of Lighthouse Keepers' Archivist, and Robbie Goldsmith for they not only provided invaluable assistance but were also kind enough to read all or parts of the manuscript and as a result put me right on a number of factual matters. Pat Walker helped me with some essential translations. I am also indebted to Barry Hawkins who in addition to providing assistance and photographs from his private collection also painted Les Hanois Lighthouse especially for this publication. Last, but certainly not least, I happily acknowledge the help and encouragement of my wife, Christine, who – as always – supported and assisted me during the long hours of research and drafting. To all the above, and many more, I owe so much. However, the responsibility for imperfections is mine, and mine alone.

Les Hanois Lighthouse - Essential Facts*

Status
Rock station

Building
Circular grey granite tower

Position
49° 26.2' N 02° 42.1' W

Established
1862

Height of Tower
33 metres

Height of Light above Mean High Water
33 metres

Automated
1996

Optic
4th order (250mm focal length) rotating optic

Lamp
35 watt metal arc lamp

Character
White group flashing twice every 13 seconds.
Blank ark: 57° (from 237° to 294°)

Intensity
89,900 candela

Range of Light
20 nautical miles

Fog signal character
Sounding twice every 60 seconds
(blast: 3.0 secs; silent 2.0 secs; blast: 3.0 secs; silent 52 secs)

Fog signal range
Two nautical miles
****

* Relevant information in 2003.

CHAPTER ONE

HIDDEN HAZARDS

An air of menace surrounds the jagged outcrop of rocks, extending just over one and a half nautical miles off the western point of Guernsey. These are "Les Hanois", described by Victor Hugo as having been "guilty of all the evil deeds of which rocks are capable".

The very name "Hanois" is darkly descriptive. In his scrapbook, the late Guernsey writer Carol Toms asserted the word meant "agony" in Celtic. The linguistic history "The Ancient & Modern Names of the Channel Islands" by Richard Coates says the derivation may well be "the wraiths" – a spectre or ghost – in Guernsey French.

The rocks carry their own individual identities, such as La Mauve, Les Aiguillons, Grande Boue Bissets, Cat Rock, Round Rock, Heronée, Percée, Hayes Rock, and Grand Hanois itself. On a calm, sunny day they look innocently picturesque. But the reef is beguiling for it is constantly troubled by tricky currents and unpredictable seas. To return to Victor Hugo in his book "Toilers of the Sea", these rocks "are the most ruthless destroyers of the sea. They lie in a treacherous ambush for vessels in the night."

Indeed, throughout history there have been many notable shipwrecks on and around this reef; almost 120 are listed in this book. Two in particular led to a concerted – and lengthy – campaign for the construction of a lighthouse.

HMS Boreas, a 6th rate 28-gun frigate, was on an errand of mercy when she came to grief with serious loss of life in a gale on the evening of November 28th 1807. *Boreas* had sailed from St Peter Port to rescue a Rocquaine pilot cutter in difficulties in bad weather and, with boat in tow, was driven by the strong north easterly winds and a heavy swell on to the Hanois rocks. The pilots cut the towing rope and managed to sail clear but the *Boreas* was trapped and pounded to destruction.

No less than 127 men were drowned, including the 29-year old Captain, Robert Scott who was reputed to be a fine young officer. More than 70 officers and ratings were saved, many of them thanks to the knowledge and bravery of the fishermen and pilots of Rocquaine who returned to the scene at daylight. (In a letter to Trinity House written 41 years later at the height of the controversy raging about the need for a lighthouse, the Chamber of Commerce argued that one of the island's best pilots was on board the *Boreas.* This pilot had ordered the ship to be put about but the officer in command would not take it upon himself to give the necessary orders in the absence of the Captain. The ship was lost in the resultant confusion.)

HMS Boreas was one of the ships of the Channel Islands Station under the command of a distinguished Guernseyman, Vice-Admiral Sir James Saumarez. In a letter to the subsequent Court Martial, held on board *HMS Gladiator,* Sir James lamented the loss of so many brave men who had perished on this "melancholy occasion". He praised Captain Scott and all his officers and men "for their standing and good conduct under such perilous circumstances in a dark and tempestuous night in the midst of the most dangerous rocks that can be conceived".

Sir James himself was well acquainted with these dangerous rocks. Indeed, 13 years earlier he had distinguished himself in a naval action with the French off the west coast of Guernsey. Sir James was Captain of the 36-gun frigate *HMS Crescent,* commanding a small squadron that had set sail from Plymouth in a full gale. As they approached Guernsey from the North West five French frigates were spotted to the South East. Sir James ordered his smaller ships round the Hanois reef to safety while he drew the attention of the French. Under fire, and displaying considerable seamanship and bravery, Sir James then headed inshore towards rock-strewn Vazon Bay and the protection of the island's shore batteries. Sir James was fortunate enough to have at his side an old Guernsey pilot, Jean Breton, who had an intimate knowledge of the island's narrow channels and reefs. Watched by a gathering crowd the French turned tail and Sir James sailed on to meet up with the rest of the squadron safely at anchor under the guns of Castle Cornet.

The loss of *HMS Boreas* was later to be cited as a reason why a lighthouse should be built on the westerly tip of Guernsey. As if to emphasise the point a cannon, recovered from the wreck of the frigate, has been placed at the Fort Grey Shipwreck Museum in Guernsey pointing directly at the present-day lighthouse on Les Hanois.

But in truth it was the wreck of a much more humble vessel that initiated the real campaign for Les Hanois Lighthouse. That was the merchant ship, a Danish dogre named *Marie Elizabeth* from Copenhagen that came to grief on November 12th 1816. The small sailing vessel, under the command of Jans Draversen, was carrying a mixed cargo – including liquorice, sumac (the leaves of a shrub used in tanning and dyeing), lemon peel and pumice stone – from Palermo, Sicily, to Rotterdam when she was driven by strong westerly winds on to rocks at Rocquaine.

The vessel and her crew were spotted in this "perilous situation" around 5am and a local man, Pierre Gallienne and six colleagues set out in a boat to give assistance. Just as they came alongside a giant wave wrenched five of the oars from the rescuers' hands, forcing them to return to shore for replacements. They put out to sea again, this time with another boat belonging to Thomas Le Huray. In spite of the appalling conditions they were successful in rescuing the seven crew from the wrecked dogre.

The *Gazette de Guernesey* four days later called on the Guernsey authorities to generously compensate these local men, most of whom were poor fishermen, who had risked their lives to save the ill-fated shipwrecked mariners. The rescued crew, having come from the Mediterranean, were subject to quarantine restrictions and placed in Rocquaine Castle (now called Fort Grey) for the requisite period. The newspaper commented that as soon as Guernsey's Lieutenant Governor, Major-General Henry Bailey, learned of this unfortunate event – and "with his habitual humanity" – he sent refreshment to the quarantined crew. Much of the cargo was salved and auctioned off a few weeks later.

Twelve days after the wreck of *Marie Elizabeth* the *Gazette* carried a letter to the editor penned by 'Humanitas' in which he, or she, called for the erection of a lighthouse in the west of the island.

The letter, addressed to Guernsey's civic leaders, started in a sensible way, praising the many improvements made to the island through their ministry – such as the prison, the roads and banks. It then continued:

"Allow me to put before you something that has struck me for many years and that the shipwreck of the night of the 11 and 12 of this month has reinforced. It is of the absolute necessity (in my opinion) to construct a lighthouse on the Plainmont heights. Hardly a winter passes without several vessels being smashed on those enormous rocks to the west of the island. Sometimes it happens that the

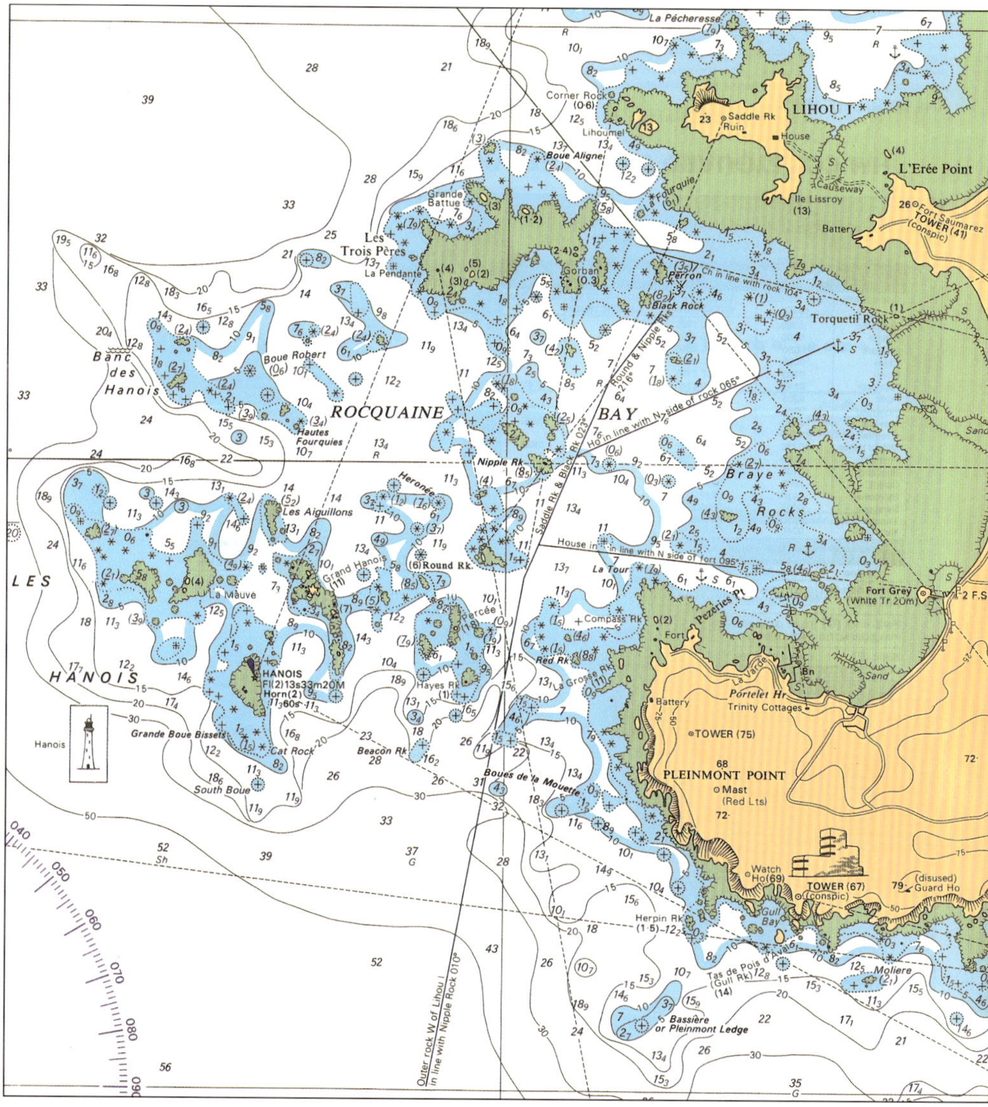

4. The hazards around Les Hanois. Reproduced from Admiralty chart SC 807 by permission of the Controller of Her Majesty's Stationery Office and the UK Hydrographic Office (www.ukho.gov.uk).

5. A "new" map of Guernsey, first published in 1794, just 13 years before the frigate HMS Boreas was wrecked on Hanois rocks. No less than 127 men drowned in the tragedy which led to a campaign for the installation of a lighthouse off the island's west coast.

men are saved, but that is not always the case: often debris or some of the cargo is found while nothing is known of the fate of the people. That spot is infamous for storms. The lives of our fellow creatures should be as dear to us as the loss of a piece of land, and thus we should do our very best to conserve life."

'Humanitas' ended by suggesting it was probable that given the loss of *HMS Boreas* in these waters, the Lords of the Admiralty might be among those who would willingly support such a "noble project".

This appeal for a lighthouse was not before time given the wrecks that had occurred and the continuing dangers to shipping that was so evident. After all warning lights had been shining since 1724 at the Casquet Rocks, a dangerous reef off the west coast of Alderney to the north of Guernsey. These coal-fired lights had resulted from a petition to the Court of Trinity House signed by 800 merchants and ship owners and prompted by the owner of the rocks, Thomas Le Cocq, an Alderney magistrate. They were all concerned about the repeated accidents that were occurring there.

Le Cocq was granted a patent in the name of Trinity House and he built and maintained the lights under a 61-year lease. The owners of English vessels paid dues of one half-penny per ton every time their vessels passed the Casquets beacon on outward or homeward journeys. The dues were doubled for owners of foreign vessels. These tariffs were to figure prominently in the debate – much later – on whether or not the Hanois lighthouse should be erected.

Three lights called St Peter, St Thomas, and Dungeon were set up in a triangular pattern on the Casquets to make them distinguishable from any of the warning lights on the nearby French coast. When Le Cocq's lease expired in October 1785 Trinity House assumed control of the lights and five years later they were converted to oil lit Argand lamps with metal reflectors.

Prompted by the wreck of *Marie Elizabeth* (incidentally called *Maria Elizabeth* in the *Gazette de Guernesey*) and, perhaps by the pleas of the mysterious "Humanitas", Major General Bailey immediately wrote to Trinity House calling for the installation of a lighthouse.

The Lieutenant Governor's plea received surprising short shrift when it was considered by Trinity House on January 23rd 1817. The minutes of that meeting, attended by 18 brethren and chaired by Captain Joseph Cotton, Deputy Master, makes fascinating reading in the light of what happened decades later.

The minutes show that Major General Bailey's letter, read by the brethren, had represented the recent loss of vessels off the "south west end" of Guernsey and the "great utility and importance (in his opinion) of a light to warn ships of their danger being placed on the heights of Pleinmont, the nearest headland to the Hannaway Rocks".

After due consideration, it was ordered that a letter should be written back to the Governor. It had been concluded that "a light in the situation so proposed is unnecessary, the lights at Portland and the Caskets being sufficient guides for the navigation thro' that part of the channel, and to guard against the danger complain'd of. And moreover a light so placed, from its liability to be mistaken for the lights in the vicinity would probably be productive of much greater mischief to the general trade passing up and down Channel than it could possibly prove of benefit to the local navigation of those islands."

But Trinity House seems to have missed the point. Those who were calling for a lighthouse were not doing so in the interests of "local navigation". Guernsey traders, pilots and fishermen were well aware of the dangers lurking among the island's reefs and channels. The campaigners' interests lie with those less familiar with the island's hazards; those mariners passing the west coast on their way to and from foreign ports.

Nevertheless the Court of Trinity House had made it clear it considered that a lighthouse at Les Hanois would do more harm than good. It seemed that the campaign had been strangled at birth.

Over the following decades there were further wrecks to confirm the perils of the Hanois rocks, among them *La Rose Victoire,* from Honfleur in France,in 1820, the schooner *Buccleugh* in 1834 and the *George William* in 1835. And clearly quiet pressure for a lighthouse continued to be exerted for in 1847 representatives from Trinity House visited Guernsey.

A Trinity House Committee minute of June 1847 indicates that there had been a distinct change of heart at the Corporation following the curt rejection of 1815. The Corporation now seemed to be advocating the erection of a lighthouse.

The minute says that Sir William Francis Patrick Napier, the Lieutenant Governor, had told the representatives that there was nothing in the constitution of the island to require Trinity House to apply for the erection of a lighthouse. Nor was there anything to prevent Her Majesty Queen Victoria granting a patent for a toll to cover maintenance costs. However, the Chamber of Commerce had made it plain that it was the "decided opinion of all the shipowners at Guernsey" that such a light was unnecessary and that they would consider it "a grievance" to be taxed to pay any portion of the expense.

So in the intervening years the protagonists and antagonists appear to have changed ends. A new, intense – and at times highly acrimonious – episode in the campaign for Les Hanois Lighthouse was about to begin.

6. This model of a lighthouse keeper, looking uncannily like Robbie Goldsmith in his days at Les Hanois, is displayed at the Fort Grey Shipwreck Museum in Guernsey. (Robbie Goldsmith)

7. One of the cannons from HMS Boreas, a 28-gun frigate, that was wrecked on the Hanois rocks in 1807 in a ferocious storm. No less than 127 men were drowned. The tragedy was one of the incidents that led to a long and concerted campaign for the construction of a lighthouse off Guernsey's west coast. Appropriately the cannon, displayed at the Fort Grey Shipwreck Museum, points directly at Les Hanois lighthouse. (Author)

8. Stores being delivered to the pre-modernised Les Hanois lighthouse by a whaler that was previously a lifeboat on the wrecked steamer ss Briseis The steamer, which was carrying 7,000 casks of Algerian wine, sank in October 1937 after striking a reef off Vazon Bay on Guernsey's west coast. Her crew of 27 managed to land safely in two lifeboats. However, the wreck became famous for the impromptu party that followed as the casks of wine began floating ashore. A local newspaper described the spectacle: "Amazing scenes of drunkenness, free fights and encounters with the law were witnessed... Men pounced on the barrels as they came in, broached them and licked up the fluid as it streamed out. Some of the elite even brought wineglasses to sample the liquid." (Guernsey Press)

CHAPTER TWO

CONCERTED CAMPAIGN

By this time a particularly persuasive and energetic pro-lighthouse campaigner had emerged. He was Captain William Sadler, a resident of Stonehouse in Gloucestershire but, more to the point, master of the little steamer *Sir Francis Drake* which regularly sailed between Plymouth and the Channel Islands in the 1828-1858 period. He was fully conversant with the hazards and the challenges to mariners navigating around Guernsey as he demonstrated in a letter to Trinity House in February 1848.

The letter, copied to Guernsey Chamber of Commerce, was prompted by the wreck of the *Emmanuel,* a barque that had struck Les Grunes de Nord-Ouest, about five nautical miles north west of Les Hanois, at midnight on January 30th that year. The vessel had been bound from Quebec to Hull and was about to enter the English Channel when she came to grief. Fortunately for the crew the *Emmanuel* was laden with timber. Capt Sadler pointed out that if she had been laden with any other description of cargo all hands would have perished for within 10 minutes of striking the rocks the vessel was full of water.

In a style that was to become familiar with various authorities, Capt Sadler deployed in argument his considerable experience in navigating this coastal area. In empathising with the *Emmanuel's* crew, he wrote that their statement indicated that a few minutes before they struck Les Grunes they had seen the lights of the Casquets. As they had not seen Guernsey they had fully expected the lights to be those of Portland. Very naturally they had kept the ship away, on a Channel course.

"The Caskets bear by compass from the Grunes about ENE 15 or 16 miles. No doubt this man fancied himself some distance from the English coast and was steering in about ENE to endeavour to sight Portland." Capt Sadler added that by following this course the *Emmanuel* would have struck other rocks to the east, even if they had missed Les Grunes.

"This is a very strong proof that what I have been endeavouring to convince the whole shipping interest of Great Britain is no fiction. That an immense sacrifice of life and property does take place of various periods that is never accounted for – for the want of a light upon the Western sea shore of Guernsey. I think the subject deserves the serious consideration of those in whom the vested rights are placed to use all lawful means to protect the lives of those who have to seek their bread afloat, leaving property out of the question."

We shall hear more from Capt Sadler for he was most persistent in his letter writing – to Trinity House, the Guernsey Chamber of Commerce, the newspapers, mutual assurance companies and even the Bishop of Winchester.

An urgency was now being injected into the debate, as the local newspaper, *The Comet* recognised. It reported on March 23rd 1848 that Trinity House had contacted both the Chamber of Commerce and the Mutual Insurance Society for Guernsey Shipping about the necessity of erecting a lighthouse on Pleinmont "with a view to prevent shipwrecks on our dangerous coast". The newspaper accepted that a "great diversity of opinion exists among nautical men, as to whether the erection of a lighthouse in that locality would not rather be injurious than otherwise to vessels coming up Channel, by which the light might be mistaken for some of the lights on the English coast". Rather grandly, the newspaper added: "At present we offer no opinion on either side of the question, but may do so hereafter."

It was only a few days later that *The Comet* jumped off the fence. It did so in a lengthy, powerful editorial which is worthy of being reproduced in full:

"It is not perhaps generally known, that Mr W SADLER, commander of the Sir Francis Drake (s), has for some time been unremitting in his endeavours to induce the maritime interest of Guernsey to make application to the Elder Brethren of Trinity House for the erection of a lighthouse on Pleinmont. Captain SADLER adduces a powerful argument in support of his project. Numerous lives have at various periods been sacrificed on the south-west coast of the island, for want (he says) of a light to guide the mariner on his way up channel; and he argues that, so long as nothing is done to point out at night the dangers of our western shore, similar casualties may again occur. Recent

9. Les Hanois lighthouse at sunset. (R Tostevin)

shipwrecks, attended with a melancholy destruction of life, have fortified this opinion; and he has therefore been induced again to refer the important subject to the Trinity Board for consideration. The result has been a communication from the Board to the Chamber of Commerce and the Mutual Insurance Society for Shipping, to which allusion has already been made in our column. A general meeting of the last-named society is convened for Thursday next, to decide upon the nature of the reply to be returned thereto.

"But 'Who shall decide when doctors disagree?' The enquiry was seldom more pertinent than in the controversy between Captain SADLER and some of the members of the shipping interest. By the former it is argued that a lighthouse on Pleinmont-point would afford an eminent safeguard against the destruction of property and human life. The latter, on the other hand, contend that its erection might prove a source of calamity of far greater extent – leading mariners astray, under various circumstances, and particularly from the danger of one light being mistaken for another. The parties join issue, but on principles totally opposite. Both are anxious for the security of human life: their opinions however are 'wide as the poles asunder' in regard to the means to secure so important an object. The advocates of the measure reason from experience and argue upon fact. Experience is a great moral teacher, and facts are proverbially 'stubborn things'. Hence, it must be confessed, they adduce tangible evidence in support of their claims. They cite numerous cases of shipwrecks which at different periods have occurred in that particular locality, and arguing from cause to effect, they infer that similar disasters may again and frequently occur. The inference may be just. On the contrary, the arguments adduced against the measure are for the most part hypothetical, being chiefly grounded on the possible consequences that may ensue from the erection of a lighthouse in the locality indicated.

"We know not whether, in order to defeat the project, the fears presaged in regard to the future will be suffered to prevail over the unambiguous experience of the past. It nevertheless appears to us, that the claims of humanity should have no inconsiderable influence in the decision of this most important question. Pecuniary considerations we have purposely kept out of view, desiring rather to look at the subject in its more momentous aspect. Human life is entitled to protection at our hands; and if it be once proved that the safety of individuals is endangered by the want of a beacon-light on our coast, that circumstance must be held paramount to every other consideration. The result being now in a great

measure left in the hands of the Mutual Insurance Society, we have no doubt that its members will narrowly investigate all the arguments that may be adduced for and against the measure, and finally come to a decision which they may conceive to be most in accordance with the claims of humanity. Two conflicting principles will present themselves before these gentlemen in the discussion and may embarrass the settlement of this question. Duty and interest may materially influence their councils (sic) either way. On so nice a point, left as it is to the arbitration of the parties more immediately interested, it is no easy matter to predicate how the scale may be made to turn. There is, however, one consideration which should be steadily kept in view. It is this. The question concerns not merely the island shipping, but the shipping of all nations. Nay! Guernsey seamen themselves have an immense stake in the project before us – to say nothing of the capital embarked in our shipping. These are weighty considerations which, we feel assured, will receive all the attention that the nature of the subject unquestionably demands."

The general meeting of the Guernsey Mutual Insurance Society referred to in this editorial did in fact take place. The members duly considered a letter from the Board of Trinity House extolling the desirability of a lighthouse at Pleinmont Point. Shipowners, independent of those in the Society, were also invited to put their points of view. But the Society could not make up its mind; a vote resulted in a stale-mate. Then, as *The Comet* put it: "...one of the gentlemen in favour of a lighthouse changed sides and the question was thus negatived by a majority of one".

The editorial and that vote brought an almost immediate – and perhaps predictable – response from Capt Sadler. Writing from the *Sir Francis Drake* in Guernsey Roads the captain maintained that one fact worth more than a thousand assertions had afforded "painful corroboration" of his argument.

That very day, April 14th , news had reached St Helier in Jersey of the loss of a valuable East Indiaman with at least 11 lives. The vessel – the *Nabob* – had been blown on to Ecréhos rocks, off the north-east cost of Jersey, after encountering a heavy gale. Capt Sadler envisaged that the ship, homeward bound from Calcutta and steering a Channel course, not having obtained a navigation observation or seen land for several days, ran ashore during the night. The letter continued:

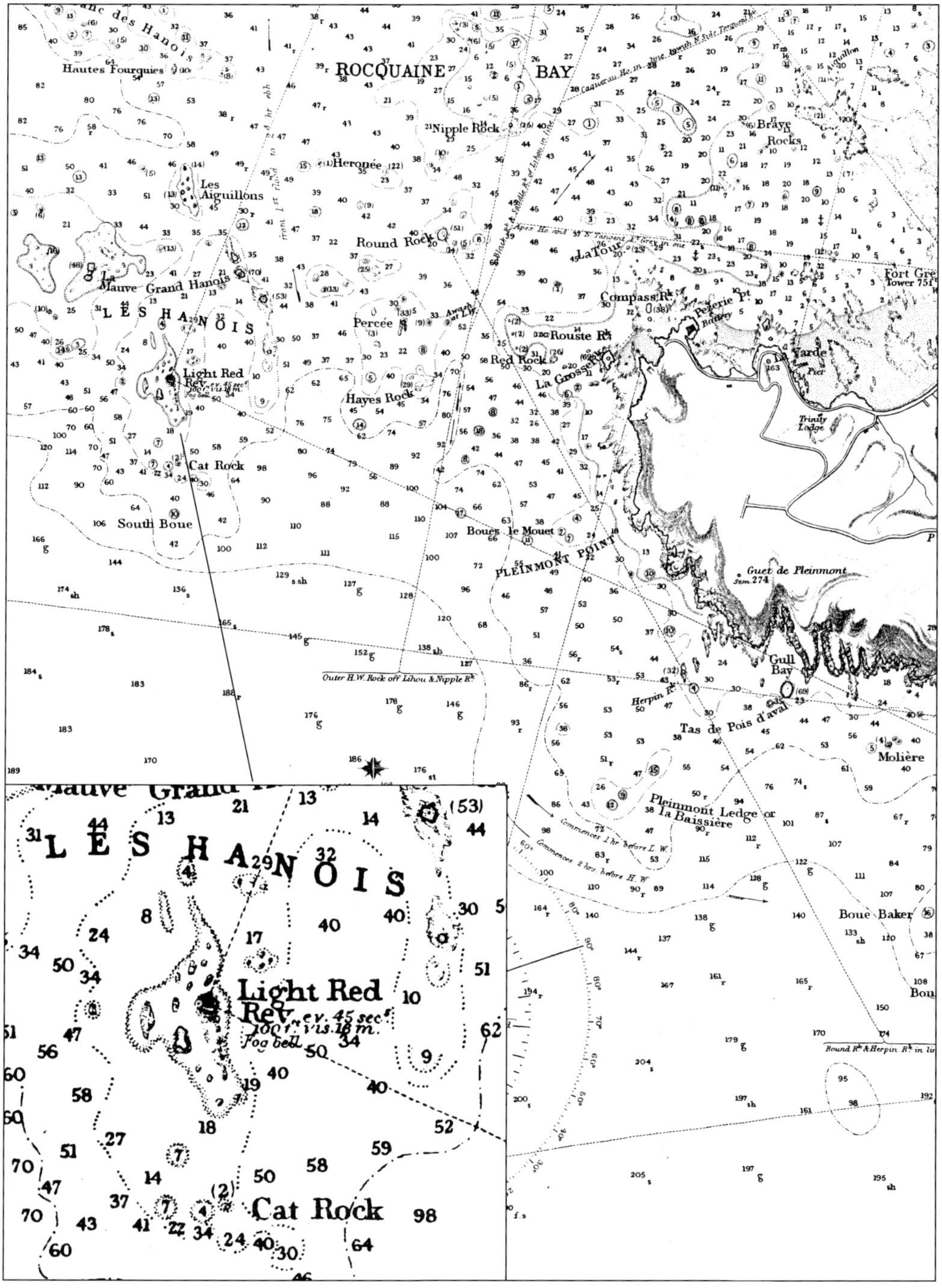

10. A portion of an Admiralty Chart of the 1860s indicating the original red light of Les Hanois lighthouse. (States of Guernsey Island Archives Service)

"It is therefore more than probable that, had there been a light on the west end of Guernsey, the ship would not have been lost. For this reason. The night was neither very dark nor very thick. And the light would have been seen above the horizon for a run of thirty miles.

"After the numerous shipwrecks that have occurred through the same cause, the present disaster requires no further comment. How long will such warnings remain unheeded? How long will life and property be periled – the interest of commerce and the rights of humanity be disregarded – for want of a beacon to warn and guide the mariner in his intricate navigation along your shore? Some of your own shipping may yet be sacrificed; and then perhaps, you gentlemen who 'sit at home at ease' may recognise the dangers that beset your coast – then you may be prompted to wipe off the stain that rests upon your character as a maritime people."

The campaign was not only becoming more vitriolic, it was also becoming more urgent for at about this time another ship had come to grief. She was the brig *Five Sisters* from Glasgow that was found wrecked on rocks in Perelle Bay, on Guernsey's West Coast. She was sailing from Lisbon to Wick with a cargo of salt, cork, wine and brandy when she came to grief. The bodies of five of the crew were picked up in a "dreadfully mutilated condition" according to the *Guernsey Sun.* These bodies were later buried in St Saviour's churchyard on the island... but only after the owners of the building in which the corpses were being kept had charged curious onlookers a fee to view the unfortunate victims.

Another local newspaper, *The Star,* reported that after inspection it was concluded that the *Five Sisters* had been out in her reckoning when she struck the rocks. Her hawse holes had been stopped from within when it was a rule for all vessels approaching the Channel to have these holes free with cables at the ready. This information only added to the clamour for a lighthouse on Guernsey's western extremity.

Not that the Chamber of Commerce was in any mood to lessen its opposition to the proposed light, as a letter of April 1st 1848 to Trinity House clearly indicates. The letter started by pointing out that the wreck of the *Emmanuel* – caused by the crew having mistaken the Casquets lights for those of Portland – had clearly demonstrated that mistakes of a similar nature would occur with a light on the South West point of Guernsey being taken for a light on the English coast. As a result, the letter says, vessels would be sent to "certain destruction on either of these islands, islets or rocks which abound in this vicinity, accelerated by the strong indraught in the Gulf of Avranches in which case the evil would predominate over any advantages that might be desired".

(Perhaps somewhat embarrassingly for the Chamber this viewpoint was contradicted a few weeks later when the Master of the *Emmanuel,* George J Burn, told readers of *The Comet* that "had such a light existed I would have seen it and thus been able to avoid the danger". Captain Burn went on: "To the want of a light, therefore, I may attribute my misfortune in striking... Since that period two vessels have been lost on the coast, both attended with great loss of life; which accidents like my own, would probably not have occurred had there been a light on Guernsey.")

The Chamber of Commerce had a different viewpoint as its own letter to Trinity House illustrates: "The loss of *Five Sisters* was a fatal event and to be deplored but it is impossible to prove the state of the ship when it drove on the rocks. She might have been disabled as to render it out of possibility to bear off a lee shore and a light in that case would not have saved her. In those heavy gales which occurred at that period the amount

11. A seagull's eye view of the Trinity House flag flying under the helideck of Les Hanois lighthouse. (Robbie Goldsmith)

of loss was immense as well as on the coasts of England even in sight of or near light houses."

12. Principal Keeper Paul Stafford photographed in the Les Hanois lighthouse service room with a lamp in 1982. (Guernsey Press)

The letter goes on:

"We object to the light on the South West point of the island on principle and for the sake of humanity because our opinion is that such a light would prove a trap to draw vessels to their destruction in the Gulf of Avranches and cause more loss to lives and property in one winter than all what has occurred on the coasts of this island in 20 years. The former cases alluded to by Capt Sadler were gross misrepresentation or exaggerations – the loss of the Sisters is almost a solitary instance...

"Nearly the whole of the island shipping is mutually insured by respective owners to the amount of above £100,000 many of whom have their sons and near relatives as part of the crews of their vessels. Therefore, if they thought that the light was necessary to the safety of the shipping they would promote instead of opposing it. No island or British vessel has been lost without recollection through the want of such a light and of the loss of the Five Sisters no clear account can be given, but an error in her supposed position is evident."

Again *The Comet* leapt to the defence of Capt Sadler – "the philanthropy of his motives cannot be questioned", it wrote. It supported the call for a lighthouse – "it is a Christian obligation to afford the required security". And it brought out into the open the real, underlying reason for the opposition to a light – money. It pointed out that pounds, shillings and pence provided the chief obstacle – "that potent spell in the way of all arrangement". The newspaper then mounted its high horse: "Such considerations become insignificant compared with the higher and nobler interests involved. We must be just before being generous; and the sentiment is perfectly rational that we cannot enjoy a privilege at the expense of the lives and properties of other people. In short, if humanity demand the sacrifice, we should make a cheerful surrender of such immunities."

It was about this time – in June 1848 – that the Reverend Daniel Dobrée, Rector of Torteval Church in Guernsey, put forward a novel solution to the impasse. He suggested in a letter to Trinity House that a light should be exhibited at the top of the Torteval church steeple. The tall spire of the Parish Church of St Philippe de Torteval is a prominent landmark at the south western end of the island; indeed even today the spire – at 105 metres – is shown on Admiralty charts as a navigational mark.

The idea clearly lingered within Trinity House for the following year the Board itself proposed that a steeple light might be a cost effective alternative to a lighthouse. In his Early History of the Hanois Lighthouse, published by La Société Guernesiaise in 1960, historian J M David wrote that the steeple light would have cost only £100. "Compared to the lighthouse which was eventually built, this seems rather reminiscent of the gentleman who, in the 1890's, opined that all the telephoning which Guernsey would ever need could be done with a speaking trumpet from Victoria Tower."

In truth the Torteval church option was never a serious contender. A visiting committee from Trinity House found the church "wholly unsuitable for the exhibition of a light for shipping". But perhaps the proposal served to provide further illustration that the controversy surrounding the construction of a lighthouse had as much to do with money as safety; in particular who was to pay the dues to fund the proposed lighthouse.

Letter writer "W.G." put his finger on the key issue in the June 12th 1848 issue of *The Comet.* "The light can be of little utility to the island shipping; but to the vessels bound up Channel from foreign ports, it will often be a great boon. Some hundreds of ship owners and shipmasters in England have signed petitions to the Trinity Board to that effect, and will never object to a light due, which would contribute so much to the safety of their lives and property. The principal part of the commerce of this island lies between London and the north of England, so that vessels employed in that trade will derive no benefit from the light and should be exempt from the tax; but those of our vessels bound to the westward will of course be subject to the toll as well as all vessels bound up or down Channel, for whose special protection the light has been advocated." The writer ends with a plea that "humanity" calls for a lighthouse. "I am sure our ship owners will not stand in the way of affording protection to the valuable class of men employed afloat."

The letter was well timed for W.G. must have been aware that the Chamber of Commerce had convened a public meeting of merchants and ship owners for a few days hence, on June 15th 1848. That meeting turned out to be one of the most remarkable episodes in this whole saga.

CHAPTER THREE

"THE FRIENDS OF DARKNESS"

The meeting, held at the Douzaine-room, was attended by about 40 merchants, ship owners and interested parties. John Valrent was asked to be chairman for what transpired to be an extraordinary discussion.

It started with the consideration of another Trinity House plea for a lighthouse, this time addressed to the newly appointed Lieutenant Governor Major General Sir John Bell. Minutes of that meeting, held in the States Archives, show that those attending recognised the matter to be "of the greatest importance in every point of view, particularly to us as ship owners".

Messrs Thomas Burley and John Jones were among those who argued against the lighthouse on the grounds that it would lead to far greater destruction of property and life than had previously occurred. It was contended that it would be an act of "suicide" to erect such a light.

On the other hand, Peter Collas, the Deputy Harbourmaster, Captain James Bienvenu and a Mr John Russell argued that a light at Pleinmont would be advantageous and of considerable importance to shipping.

It was then resolved by a majority of 21 against nine that the meeting "feeling the deep importance of the case before it cannot approve nor recommend the erection of a lighthouse on the SW point of Guernsey from a firm conviction that a light so placed would be a source of mischief and disastrous in its consequences to the homeward bound foreign shipping of this and other European countries".

Nine reasons were given for this decision:

1st. That in strong westerly gales and thick hazy weather, or otherwise in hazy weather alone, a ship entering the Channel is often many days deprived of a meridian or other altitude of the sun to determine the correct latitude of the ship, and from the same cause is prevented obtaining sights of the sun to determine the correct longitude.

2nd. That owing to the always long prevailing westerly winds, and consequent heavy western sea, combined with the strong south-east current across the Bay of Biscay, ships under those circumstances are in most cases ahead of the most careful and correct navigator.

3rd. That from 50 to 70 miles west, and in the latitude of Guernsey, there is a strong indraught into the Gulf of Avranches, the flood running for at least nine hours to a ship bound up Channel in a south-easterly direction.

4th. That in strong westerly gales it often occurs that from the absence of an altitude of the sun, ships do not make the English coast as early as ought to be the case, and being much further east as well as south from the course before adverted to, and actually in the latitude of Guernsey, whereas it is supposed they are in a fair mid-Channel course.

5th. That a vessel not having made the English coast; and being on the look-out for it, whilst on the contrary it were in the latitude of Guernsey and under the influence of a strong flood which at spring tides runs at least at the rate of six or seven miles an hour to the south east, such ship, seeing a light, would necessarily suppose it to be, possibly, Scilly, the Lizard, the Eddystone, the Start, or Portland, never contemplating for a moment being in the latitude of Guernsey.

6th. That a ship making what was supposed to be one of the afore-named lights would necessarily haul to the southward, or steer a Channel course, as the case may be; but if, unfortunately, the light seen should prove to be one on Pleinmont-point, such ship would of course haul to the southward, steering the usual Channel course, and would ere long be carried by the current among the groups of islands, islets and rocks situated in this part of the Channel.

7th. That a ship unfortunately mistaking a light on Pleinmont-point for one on the English coast must of necessity prove fatal in some way or other; for if by any chance she escape the islets and rocks, which is improbable, she will find herself on the coast of France, and there strand, as in a north-west gale it is

13. A photograph of a 1862 drawing of Les Hanois lighthouse, kept by the States of Guernsey Island Archives Service. (Author)

morally impossible to work out of any part of this Gulf.

8th. That from the preceding causes and the mistaking a light on Pleinmont-point for one of the English coast, awful must be the catastrophe for in nine cases out of ten it cannot otherwise than prove fatal to the unwary navigator.

9th. That a light on Pleinmont-point would be serviceable to the coasting trade or to ships having made the English coast is too true to be controverted. It must nevertheless be admitted that the coasting trade of the island is manned by efficient pilots and it may occur that such a light might have the effect of causing negligence on the part of the crews, moreover the western coasting trade is of little importance there being only two or three vessels trading to the island.

The meeting's decision brought the inevitable response – and a point-by-point rebuttal of the nine reasons – from Capt Sadler. Writing from his ship in Guernsey Roads he poured scorn on the 21 men who had voted against a lighthouse, describing them as "Friends of Darkness" who had laid down the "Nine Articles of their Faith". In a letter to the editor of *The Comet* Capt Sadler maintained that it was "absolutely futile" that the nine reasons had been used against the necessity of a lighthouse; in his "humble opinion" they should have been more rationally employed in the argument for a light to be erected on Pleinmont 50 years previously. He took particular exception to the 9th point that a light might cause negligence on the part of crews. "You must tell that to the marines: sailors won't believe it. I hope for the honour of the profession that no sailor had any share in the concoction of such a calumny by implication."

Trinity House minutes show that the Board was being bombarded with letters about the proposed lighthouse – from among others the Lieutenant Governor, the Chamber of Commerce and, of course, Capt Sadler (several in his case). As a result the Board decided to refer the matter to the Deputy Master, Wardens and Examining Committee.

While members of the Guernsey Chamber of Commerce remained opposed to the light, their counterparts in the neighbouring island of Jersey were being much more positive about the proposals. As if to thumb their noses at Guernsey – given the inter-island rivalry, not for the first or last time – the Jersey Chamber of Commerce unanimously passed a resolution in favour of the light. There was a condition to this backing, however. Jersey's Chamber made it plain that the island's ship owners would not expect to pay dues towards lights in the United Kingdom.

This condition was at the heart of concerns of the Channel Islands' shipping fraternity. At the time their foreign shipping paid no light dues and they were concerned that the erection of a lighthouse on Guernsey would bring them into the system.

14. The original fog bell hanging from the summit of Les Hanois lighthouse, photographed in 1962. Two years later, when the tower was completely modernised, the bell was removed and replaced with an electric fog horn. (Guernsey Press)

But about this time another obstacle seemed to present itself. Given the petitions and general clamour for the light, the Board of Trinity House had wisely sought legal opinion on its authority and abilities to erect lighthouses in the Channel Islands. The Trinity House minutes of November 14th 1848 show that the Board's counsel, Frederick Robinson, had concluded in a lengthy opinion, that "the Corporation of Trinity House has not, under its present powers, the right of erecting and maintaining light houses or beacons on the Channel Islands, and of selecting and taking the ground requisite for the buildings". On the face of it this appeared a somewhat strange ruling given that Trinity House had already acquired the Casquets lighthouse on Alderney – itself part of the Bailiwick of Guernsey.

It says much for the influence that the master of the *Sir Francis Drake* had assumed over the matter that the Elder Brethren decided to inform Capt Sadler personally of these legal doubts. Naturally, the Guernsey authorities were also informed about the potential legal impediment.

15. Torteval Church in Guernsey. In June 1848 its Rector, the Reverend Daniel Dobrée, suggested that instead of building a lighthouse, Trinity House should consider exhibiting a light at the top of the high church steeple. In the event Trinity House felt that the church would be "wholly unsuitable for the exhibition of a light for shipping". (Author)

There then followed an exchange of letters between Trinity House, Major General Sir John Bell, the Lieutenant Governor (as representative of the Sovereign) and Sir Peter Stafford Carey, Guernsey's Bailiff and head of the island's legislature.

In February 1849 Sir John told the Bailiff that given Trinity House's apparent lack of jurisdiction it might be worthwhile to consider means of "obviating any local objection to the Corporation's having that power conferred upon it in this particular instance". He added for good measure that he understood there were no funds in Guernsey out of which the cost of a lighthouse could be defrayed. "I conceive it could only be provided for by a tonnage duty on all vessels arriving from the United Kingdom or elsewhere in the island ports."

Sir Peter replied that the Royal Court of Guernsey had been consulted and it had been confirmed that there were no local funds for the erection of a lighthouse. He pointed to the existence of the Casquets light, adding that "should it at any time be deemed expedient to have another" a similar arrangement regarding erection and maintenance costs might be followed. The letter also returned to the contention that the case made out in favour of a new lighthouse had reference – almost exclusively – to the advantage of homeward bound vessels sailing up the Channel.

Another shipwreck hit the headlines in December that year. A packet ship, the *Oneida,* was on passage from New York to Le Havre when she was driven by high winds on to the rocks in Perelle Bay on Guernsey's west coast. Fortunately the 22 passengers and 28 crew were saved. Lamenting the loss of "so noble vessel", *The Comet* asked how the opponents of a lighthouse could claim "with such confidence" that a light on Pleinmont Point would increase rather than lessen dangers. "We cannot, for the life of us, comprehend how *light* is calculated to make a man *blind."* The newspaper sounded exasperated.

By the autumn of 1850, Sir John was also clearly becoming irritated by the ongoing debate. A letter, dated October 26th, addressed to the Bailiff, set out clearly the issues at that time. The letter contained an implied rebuke and a challenge. Moreover, it confirmed that the Chamber of Commerce's opposition had evaporated. In fact, this position was ratified when the Chamber formally reversed its previous resolution.

This is the letter:

Sir,

The erection of a Light House at or near Pleinmont having engaged public attention for some years, and the expectation being pretty generally entertained that the subject is still under consideration of the Authorities in England I think it is right to inform you that I have recently received certain information, although not officially communicated, that, as it is understood the Island of Guernsey would object to the Trinity House having the superintendence of the Light and the collection of dues for its maintenance, if dues be found necessary, this objection would at once be an obstacle to the Light being erected or kept up at the expense of the British Revenue.

It is considered therefore that the question is reduced to two points: -

1 Do the Channel Islands retain their objection to the proposed Light being placed – as all other British Lights are – under the superintendence of the Trinity House?

2 If they do retain this objection, what are they prepared to do themselves, for the erection and maintenance of the Light?

You will recollect that I addressed the Royal Court, through you, on the subject of this Light, in February or March 1849. The question then was – not the cost of the Light, but the propriety of any Light being erected. On that question I neither offered nor requested an opinion, contenting myself with laying before you the communication I had received.

It was clear, from the mass of correspondence etc which accompanied my letter that the only opposition to the proposed Light was by the then Guernsey Chamber of Commerce, on the ground that it would add to, rather than diminish, the risk of shipwreck. The present Chamber is, I believe, in favour of the project so that opposition on that ground may be considered at an end.

I am not aware that the Authorities of either Island have ever objected to the proposed Light being under the superintendence of the Trinity House, but it is clear that it is considered the project has been delayed, if not defeated, by Guernsey opposition.

Having had no instruction to address you on this subject, I leave it entirely to your consideration, merely remarking in conclusion that I should be sorry if the Authorities of Guernsey should be reproached with the failure of an enterprise such as this by reason of an opposition which, in as far as I am aware, has not yet been proved to exist.

I have the honor etc
JOHN BELL
Lieutenant-Governor

The tone of the Bailiff's response suggests that the Royal Court was surprised and somewhat chastened by Sir John's comments. It certainly moved along the debate.

Sir Peter replied that on no occasion had the Authorities of Guernsey expressed an opinion "adverse to the views of the Government with reference to the Light House". And the supposition that the island was opposed to the superintendence of Trinity House was "entirely without foundation". On the contrary the Royal Court would object in a "most decided manner" to the authority of a lighthouse being placed in any other hands.

The Bailiff added that given the precedent of the Casquets lighthouse, it should be accepted that Trinity House "has all the powers that are wanted". He went on: "I am requested by the Royal Court to observe that the Trinity House being acknowledged to have now the same power that it had when, in the reign of George I, it undertook to build the light on the Caskets, it only requires to refer to what was done in that case, in order to ascertain the course to be pursued in the present."

The positive tone of the Bailiff's response could not extinguish Guernsey's deep anxiety about the possible levy of light dues, however. Sir Peter made the point plainly: "There would indeed be an objection to dues being levied within the Island by an English Board. This is a thing that I am convinced the Island never would assent to."

This stubbornness was borne out of history. The Channel Islands were originally part of the Duchy of Normandy held by the Crown of England. When in 1204 King John lost these continental Normandy possessions he offered the Channel Islands a certain amount of freedom and autonomy in return for them remaining loyal to the Crown of England. In opposing possible dues being imposed by an English authority Guernsey was reiterating its special independence. But it was a stubbornness that was to set the tone of intransigent opposition for the next decade.

16. Keepers Alan Laing (right) and Robbie Goldsmith point out some of the details of the Hanois optic to 15-year-old Ian Davison of Mare de Carteret School, Guernsey, during a pre Christmas visit in 1988. Ian had made a special Christmas cake for the keepers and was rewarded with a tour of the lighthouse. (Guernsey Press)

CHAPTER FOUR

IT'S ALL ABOUT MONEY

By now Trinity House was hardening its position that a lighthouse was needed and should be built. During 1849 Members of the Board had sailed to Guernsey in the Trinity House yacht *Beacon.* They had met with various interested parties – including Capt Sadler – and had visited Pleinmont.

During the summer of 1851 a committee of Elder Brethren made another visit, this time in the *Vestal,* accompanied by a civil engineer from Messrs Walker and Burgess. Instead of concentrating on Pleinmont Point, on Guernsey's mainland, they examined the Hanois reef of rocks. They first landed on Grand Hanois. Then, aided by fishermen, they went by lifeboat and a small gig to a more accommodating rock (probably La Mauve) situated half a mile to the west. This, they thought, would be a preferable position for a lighthouse than the Grand Hanois.

In a letter to the Treasury, dated August 12th 1851, Trinity House reported that it favoured the construction of a stone-built lighthouse. It was estimated that the annual charge for maintaining and repairing the lighthouse would not exceed £900.

In August 1851 Sir John, the Lieutenant Governor, was able to write to the Bailiff that "Her Majesty's government is prepared to erect a Light House on the Hanois Rocks, provided the islands of Guernsey and Jersey will undertake to defray the cost of its maintenance" (up to £900 annually).

Sir John added: "The preliminary questions in regard to the desirability of the proposed Light, its site, and the means for its erection, having thus been settled, it would seem to rest entirely with the States of the two Islands whether the project is to be carried into execution."

Guernsey refused to budge. In his reply Sir Peter said the Royal Court saw no grounds to deviate from its position that the same arrangements should be applied as existed at the Casquets. To reinforce the point

Sir Peter argued: "The Royal Court has always considered that a lighthouse on the Western Coast might be advantageous to vessels passing up the Channel; but that it was a matter of very secondary importance to the shipping of this island."

Perhaps with tongue in cheek, Sir Peter wrote that the "force of this observation will be at once apparent by reference to the map. The island of Guernsey is a triangle." He went on that Hanois lay off the promontory that formed the angle to the West. The island's main harbour was located about half way along the side that faced East. The trade with Southampton and London, with the North of England for the coal, and with the Baltic for timber and corn, constituted by far the greatest part of Guernsey's maritime interest. Sir Peter continued:

"The course of vessels engaged in these several branches of trade lies wholly to the East and would derive little or no benefit from a light to the Westward. To the trade of Jersey it might be of more use, but I apprehend its chief importance would be with reference to vessels coming from distant ports and passing up the Channel. It is among such vessels that shipwrecks most frequently occur. Of all the vessels that have been wrecked upon our Western coast during a long series of years, the Court is not aware of there having ever been one that was bound for this island. The vessels that are wrecked are almost invariably vessels from a distant port bound to some port up the Channel and out of their course."

It was time for due diligence examination to be performed by interested parties. A special committee of the States of Guernsey was appointed to review the lighthouse proposal and its implications. As part of its deliberations it called on Trinity House to provide copies of all the light duties payable to the Corporation. Two months later – in April 1852 – the House of Commons called on Trinity House to supply copies of all correspondence and cost estimates pertaining to the proposed lighthouse.

The Guernsey authorities continued to dig in their heels and the debate over jurisdiction and dues dragged on. As J M David commented in his paper on the early history of the Hanois lighthouse, "every letter, every proposal was subjected by him (Sir Peter Stafford Carey, the Bailiff) to the most meticulous scrutiny and his replies and arguments are masterpieces of logical reasoning".

In a bid to draw a line under the issue the British Government announced in 1853 that it planned to insert a special clause in the Merchant Shipping Bill that was then passing through the committee

17. Les Hanois lighthouse in 1967. (Guernsey Press)

stage in the House of Commons. This clause would give Trinity House the same powers of erecting and maintaining lighthouses in the Channel Islands as existed in England. It would also enable the Queen, by Order in Council, to fix a toll to be paid by ships which passed or derived benefit from such lighthouses.

As was to be expected the Guernsey authorities were asked for their opinion on the proposals. This came, without delay, in another typical response from the Bailiff to the Lieutenant Governor:

"The Royal Court is of the opinion that there can be no objection to Light Houses in the Channel Islands being built by Trinity House and

18. Cecil Brouard, one of the crew of the Beacon, about to drop anchor off Les Hanois lighthouse in 1962. Minutes later the relieved keepers were transferred to the whaler and rowed to shore. (Guernsey Press)

placed under its superintendence. But – as I have already had occasion to state to Your Excellency – there would be strong objections to dues being levied within the Island by an English Board or by a Receiver appointed by the Government, and there would be an equally strong objection to money being raised for the purpose, otherwise than with the assent of the States."

The letter went on to question whether the true cost of maintenance and repairs would amount to the £900 estimated by Trinity House. "There exists a strong impression that it would not amount to that sum," commented the Bailiff.

Sir Peter then went on to reiterate that the proposed lighthouse would be of relatively small benefit to Guernsey's maritime trade... "Without having any statistical statements to refer to, I think that I may assert with perfect safety that of the vessels passing the Light, not one in four would come into any port in the Channel Islands and that of those bound for the Channel Islands not above one in three would enter the port of Guernsey."

Then Sir Peter put forward Guernsey's own financial proposal... "Under these circumstances the Royal Court conceives that an annual contribution of £75 would amply cover any claim that could be made upon the Island. And the Court would suggest that this sum might with propriety be charged upon the Harbour dues in the following proportions, viz: £50 a year from the Harbour of St Peter Port and £25 a year from the Harbour of St Sampson's."

Unmoved by this response, the British Government pressed ahead. In February the following year the Privy Council wrote to the Bailiff enclosing the proposed clause for the Merchant Shipping Bill. This brought a furious response from the Bailiff who claimed that it violated "the first and fundamental privilege of the inhabitants... of the most vital importance, and one that from the remotest ages to the present time has ever been held sacred and inviolate... that no taxes can be imposed... no tolls levied... no money raised by authority other than that of the inhabitants".

Faced with these arguments, based on privileges conferred in 1204, the Privy Council relented. It was agreed that no tolls could be levied without the consent of Guernsey. As a report from the States committee set up to evaluate the lighthouse proposal was to point out later: the Merchant Shipping Act, 1854, was a "most important acknowledgement of the British Parliament and of Council that the island, or the trade in the island, cannot be taxed without the consent of the States. The Act is, in this respect a renewal of our Charters, a protection for the future." But this still left open the question about who would pay for the upkeep of the proposed lighthouse. It was a question that would be asked over and over again in the coming years.

In 1857, for instance, there was an exchange of letters indicating that much had still to be resolved. Indeed, the interested parties seem to be going round in circles, revisiting positions previously settled. Guernsey Chamber of Commerce wrote to Lord Palmerston, the Prime Minister, "praying that sanction may be given for the erection of a Light House on the West Coast". The Government asked the authorities in Guernsey and Jersey how much they would be willing to contribute towards the erection and maintenance of a light house, if its construction should be considered desirable by Trinity House. And the Board of Trade asked of Trinity House for information about where the lighthouse would be erected, and how much it would cost to build and maintain.

In reply to the final point Trinity House answered that it was unable to arrive at any "definitive opinion" other than by reference to the cost of works at other lighthouses. For instance, Bishop Rock lighthouse in the Scilly Isles – the Corporation's first granite tower then under construction – would cost £34,559 when completed in 1858.

Trinity House was itself displaying signs of impatience at the ongoing arguments and uncertainties. In June 1858 it repeated a plea to the Board of Trade for the go-ahead on the Hanois project. It pointed out that construction of the Bishop Rock tower was nearing completion and would shortly enable "the removal therefrom of the person now employed thereat whose services might then be transferred to the Hanois". That person was probably James Douglass who was assisting his eminent father, Nicholas Douglass, the superintendent engineer for the Bishop Rock construction. In the event, as we will see, it was Nicholas's other lighthouse engineering son, William, who was later to be appointed in charge of the Hanois tower construction.

It was not only the money issue that was exercising the minds of Trinity House for, during this long Hanois gestation period, various proposals were submitted by well-meaning members of the public, anxious to speed things along. For instance, a chartered engineer, Alexander Gordon proposed that the lighthouse should be constructed of iron, rather than stone. There were also calls for the lighthouse to be built on Guernsey's mainland rather than on the Hanois reef. But Trinity House was clear – it wanted the lighthouse to be built either on La Mauve Rock or the nearby Le Bisseau Rock. And it wanted it built of stone. It just needed the decision to go ahead.

Guernsey was still arguing that the levying of tolls should be at the same rate and on the same terms as those applying to the Casquets lighthouse, as evidenced by a letter of July 31st 1858 from the Bailiff to the Lieutenant Governor.

At the same time neighbouring Jersey was doing its best to break the impasse. Its Bailiff, John Hammond, wrote to the British Government offering to pay £50 annually to the maintenance of Hanois light "provided the island of Guernsey contributes a like sum for such purpose". The letter suggested that contributions should cease as soon as revenues from light dues were sufficient to defray the cost of erection and maintenance.

In September the Board of Trade wrote saying that "My Lords trust that the States of Guernsey, with as little delay as possible, give an answer to the question whether they are prepared to contribute Fifty Pounds (£50) annually, in respect of such of their trade as will not pay the Toll. This contribution would be linked to a change in the status of Guernsey shipping, trading with the United Kingdom – in essence it would be treated more favourably as coasting trade rather than foreign trade."

The implied answer was simple – "No!" – although the fact that this answer was not immediately made explicit caused some later confusion over whether or not Guernsey shipping would pay the lower dues of the coasting trade.

However, the reply given in a letter from the Bailiff to the Lieutenant Governor on October 25th was typically elegant in style:

"It will be recollected that when it was proposed by Government that the Island of Guernsey should pay £50 as a contribution for its foreign trade, it was urged on behalf of the Island that, in that case, its trade with the United Kingdom should pay no higher dues than are paid by the British Coasting trade.

"The States are not left altogether without data to guide them in their judgement. We know from the Parliamentary Return that in the year 1848 the Revenue of the Caskets left a clear surplus of upwards of £5,600. The Royal Court would submit with some confidence...that a Toll much less than what was charged in respect of the Casket Lights in 1848 would produce an amount amply sufficient to cover all the expenses of the proposed Light on the Hanois....

"The demand made by the Board of Trade – correctly stated – is not that the States should vote a certain contribution towards the expense of a Light on the Hanois, but that on such a Light House being erected, they should grant certain moneys to be paid over to an aggregate Fund applicable to the General Lighthouse System of the United Kingdom.

"Their Lordships (Board of Trade) *will not lose sight of the fact that a Light on the Hanois is a thing that the States have never asked for – they having all along considered that a light might perhaps be required, as a national*

19. Les Hanois lighthouse as depicted on two Guernsey stamps – the 4p issued in 1976 and one in the "Island Colours" self-stick set issued in April 2001. (Guernsey Post Office)

20. The reverse side of the States of Guernsey £5 note showing Les Hanois lighthouse in 1862 and Fort Grey where the construction workers were accommodated. Fort Grey now houses Guernsey's Shipwreck Museum where a number of artifacts from the lighthouse are exhibited. (D M Clark, States Treasurer)

work, for the general safety of vessels passing up the Channel, but so far as trade of this island was concerned it was a matter of very secondary importance; and, in point of fact, of all the vessels that have been wrecked on the western coast within the memory of man, there has not been one that was bound for Guernsey..."

The issue was finally resolved in the early months of 1859. The British Government relented, in essence acknowledging that £50 a year was not worth fighting over. The decision is recorded in a letter from Thomas Farrar of the Board of Trade, Marine Division, to Jurat Henry Tupper, chairman of the States lighthouse committee.

The historic letter, dated March 26th 1859, stated without fanfare: "My Lords have decided to proceed with the erection of the lighthouse, levying the light dues as heretofore at the overseas rates on Guernsey and Jersey vessels in ports in the United Kingdom (including a toll for the Hanois light), without requiring any contribution from either of those towards the maintenance of the light.

"I am to add that my Lords have requested the Trinity House to proceed with the works of the Lighthouse with as little delay as possible."

The decision was also recorded in the Minutes of the Trinity House Board three days later: "It was hereupon referred to the Committee of Deputy Master and Wardens to take the necessary steps for the commencement of the works as early as may be practicable."

This then should have been the final green light for the long-overdue construction of Les Hanois lighthouse. But there was to be another twist, again concerning light dues levied on Guernsey's ships.

Henry Tupper's assiduousness and due diligence had resulted in a detailed knowledge of shipping dues in the United Kingdom. These tolls, he reported, could be summarised as the "Coasting Rates" (dues payable by vessels engaged in the coasting trade of the UK) and the "Overseas Rates" (dues payable by all vessels engaged in foreign trade).

His committee calculated that if the island trade continued under the overseas rates – as proposed by the Board of Trade – the toll for the Hanois light would be in itself nearly three times as heavy as that for vessels from the UK bound for Guernsey. Its report added: "In the present state of things, the island having but little control over the Trinity House, tolls in respect of the Hanois may be raised in the ports of the United Kingdom indiscriminately on our steam and St Sampson's traders heavier in amount than could be collected here on that trade which at present escapes altogether."

Henry Tupper reported that the Committee estimated that in respect of light dues alone the payment of the overseas rates was an annual charge on the island trade totalling £941.19s.4d. "It is no privilege to be overtaxed. Is it not, on the contrary, a privilege to be entitled to demand that a tax be reduced?"

The Committee appealed to the Board of Trade to have its island's shipping treated as coastal trade. In keeping with what had gone on over the previous decade there was a last-minute confrontation. Thomas Farrar told Henry Tupper that the island had effectively abandoned its quest for coastal trading status when it refused to make a special contribution to the upkeep of Hanois. The Board of Trade saw no reason why it should now comply with Guernsey's request.

But again there was a change of heart with Guernsey winning its way. The consequent Parliamentary Order in Council confirmed that the superintendence and management of lighthouses erected in and around Guernsey, Alderney and Sark should be vested in Trinity House. It also stated that "the trade in future from the United Kingdom to the said islands of Guernsey, Alderney and Serk (sic) and from the said islands respectively, shall be placed on the footing of a coasting trade in respect of the payment of all lights, pilotage, harbour and other local dues and tolls, and in those respects only, and that all vessels trading from the United Kingdom to the said islands respectively shall pay the coasting rates only and not the overseas rates as heretofore".

Today there are no light dues charged on vessels in Guernsey. Indeed, in a novel twist to the old argument, Trinity House pays the States of Guernsey £1,000 a year as a contribution to the maintenance of Platte Fougère light off the island's north east coast. Unlike Les Hanois, Platte Fougère is maintained by the States rather than by Trinity House. Indeed, in Guernsey this substantial beacon is reputed to be not only the world's first concrete "lighthouse" but also the first "unmanned lighthouse". It might also be deemed one of the ugliest structures of its kind. The Trinity House contribution recognises the fact that whereas Les Hanois is still regarded as purely an aid to general navigation, Platte Fougère is an aid to both general and local shipping.

But, back in the mid 19th century, the arguing was at last over. Les Hanois lighthouse could now be built.

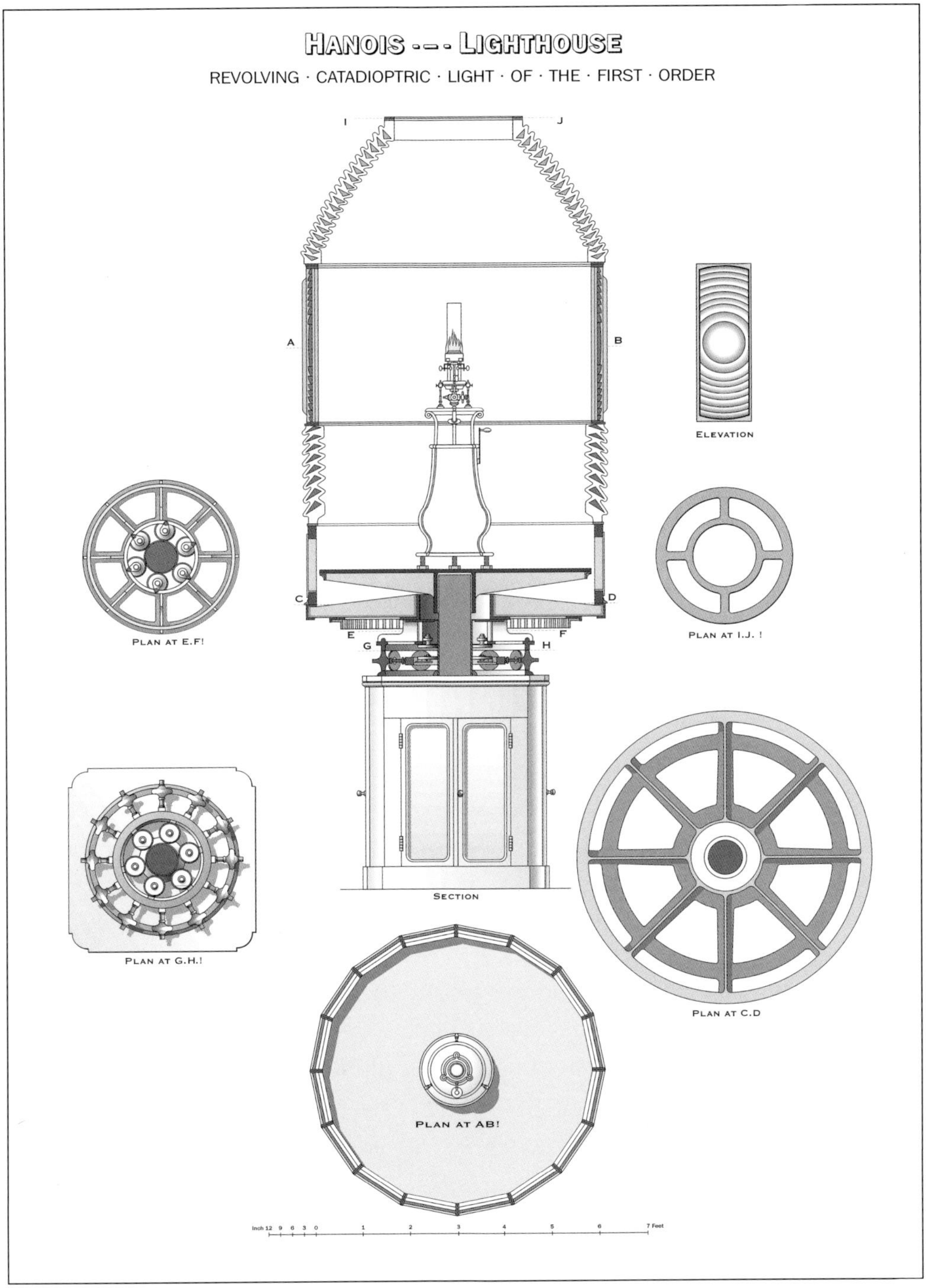

21. Drawings of the first Les Hanois light. *(Hans-Günter Spitzer)*

CHAPTER FIVE

A GRANITE MARVEL

Although the formal decision to proceed had been taken and communicated by the Board of Trade there were still some key issues to be settled. The Minutes of the Trinity House Court of March 29th 1849 records that the Corporation had been asked by the Government to commence the works "with as little delay as possible". Accordingly the matter was referred to the Committee of Deputy Master and Wardens "to take the necessary steps for the commencement of the works as early as may be practicable".

Location

For a start Trinity House had still not decided on a location – somewhat surprising given the many years of debate and a number of Corporation visits to the island. The choice was between La Roque à la Mauve – "Sea gull rock" – and Le Bisseau, also known as Grande Boue Bissets (literally "two united rocks").

In July 1858 another committee sailed in the Trinity House vessel *Argus* to inspect Les Hanois rocks. Their first stop was La Mauve, the outermost rock deemed "practicable for building on". The committee felt that La Mauve was "without doubt the best position for the Light, but surrounded as it is by sunken rocks, the difficulty of landing materials would doubtless be very great".

After careful consideration and having taken a set of angles and bearings, the committee proceeded to Le Bisseau, lying 640 yards South by East. Here, sensibly, the committee listened to the advice of a local pilot who had been asked to join them. The minutes record: "The pilot stated that the weather must be very bad when a landing could not be effected on Le Bisseau whereas the weather must be exceedingly fine to admit of landing on La Mauve." Further angles and bearings were taken which confirmed that "the advantages are in favour of La Mauve for covering the dangers to the Northward and of Le Bisseau to the Southward".

The Committee also believed that it would be easier to land supplies and effect reliefs on Le Bisseau. This consideration would "fully balance" the small natural superiority of La Mauve's position. But clearly, in the committee's eyes, there was not much to choose between the alternative locations.

It was to be several months before a decision was taken. More visits of inspection were made, including one by James Walker, the designing engineer. Then *The Comet* reported in August that "it now appears that the Besoe (Bisseau) rock and not the Gull has been selected for its erection." One of the considerations, it seems, was the amount of logistical support and ancillary construction work that would be required for the erection of a lighthouse on La Mauve or Le Bisseau. This in turn affected cost estimates. In the event – as the Board of Trade spotted – it would be cheaper to build Hanois Light on Le Bisseau than on La Mauve.

Design

Many of the key factors – the cost, location, logistical support and so forth – depended on the design of the lighthouse. Trinity House opted for a granite tower, but one with a notable difference from its predecessors.

The tower would be built to the pattern devised by Robert Stevenson, Chief Engineer to the Northern Lighthouse Board, and incorporating improvements introduced by Nicholas Douglass, Superintendent Engineer of Trinity House and John Smeaton, the noted lighthouse designer and father of British civil engineering. The light would shine from 100 feet high above the high water mark although the tip of the weather vane would raise the overall height to 117 feet.

The masonry – in total 24,542 cubic feet – would be erected 90 feet high, set firmly on a natural rock which would rise 14 feet inside the tower. The lighthouse would be 32 feet 7 inches in diameter at the base and just 17 feet at its "waist". The diameter of the light gallery course would be 20 feet 6 inches. The interior spiral staircase, seven feet in diameter, was designed to serve six rooms, the floors of each room being of radial stone, dovetailed into central stones.

The novel feature in the Les Hanois design rests with the way each of the granite blocks are fitted together. It would be the first tower where the

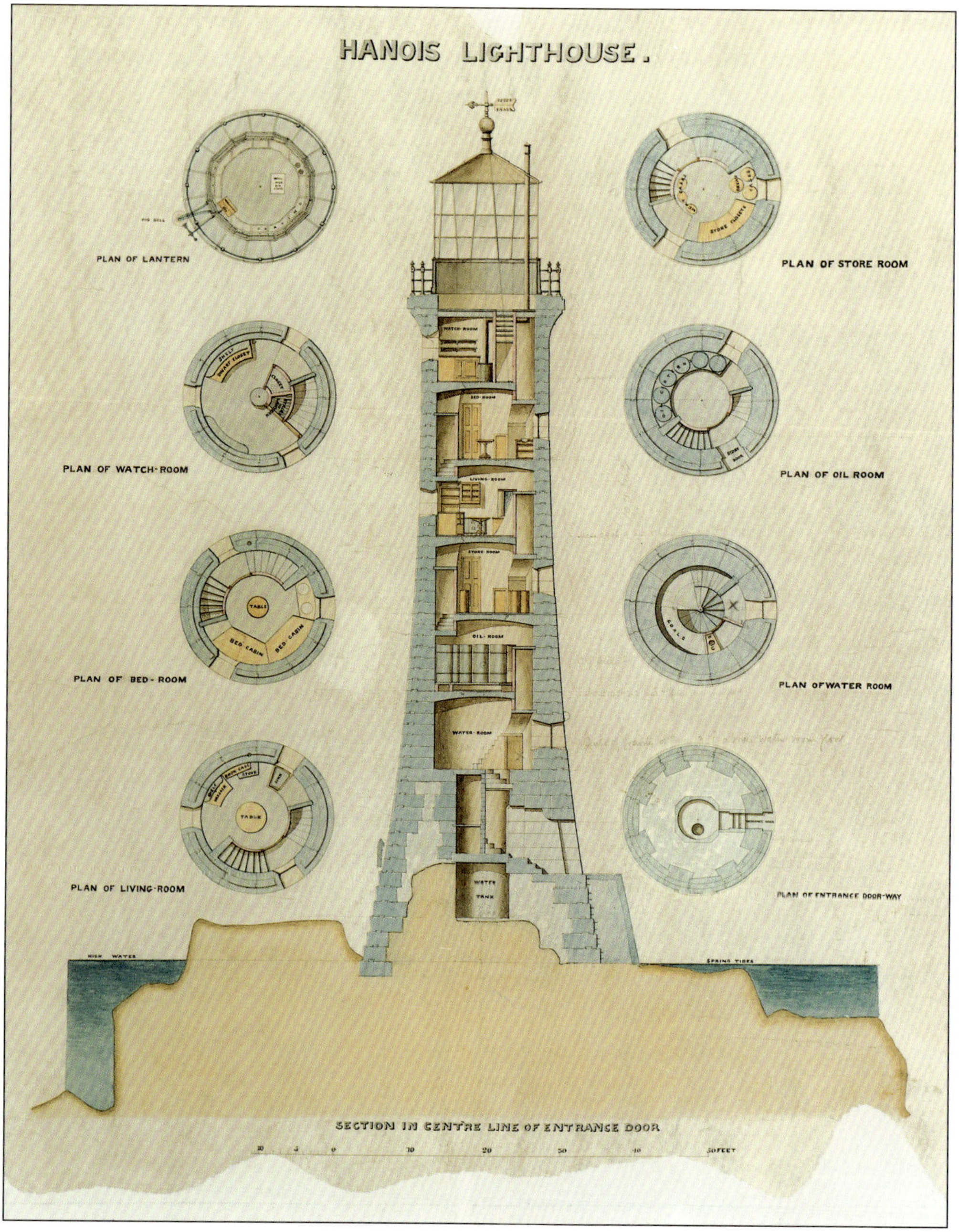

22. An 1862 section drawing of Les Hanois lighthouse – specially amended for this book – showing the lay-out of the individual rooms. It shows clearly how the tower was erected above a protruding rock on which stood the water tank. The drawing was made by Mathews, Burges and Cooper, consulting engineers to Trinity House. (Trinity House)

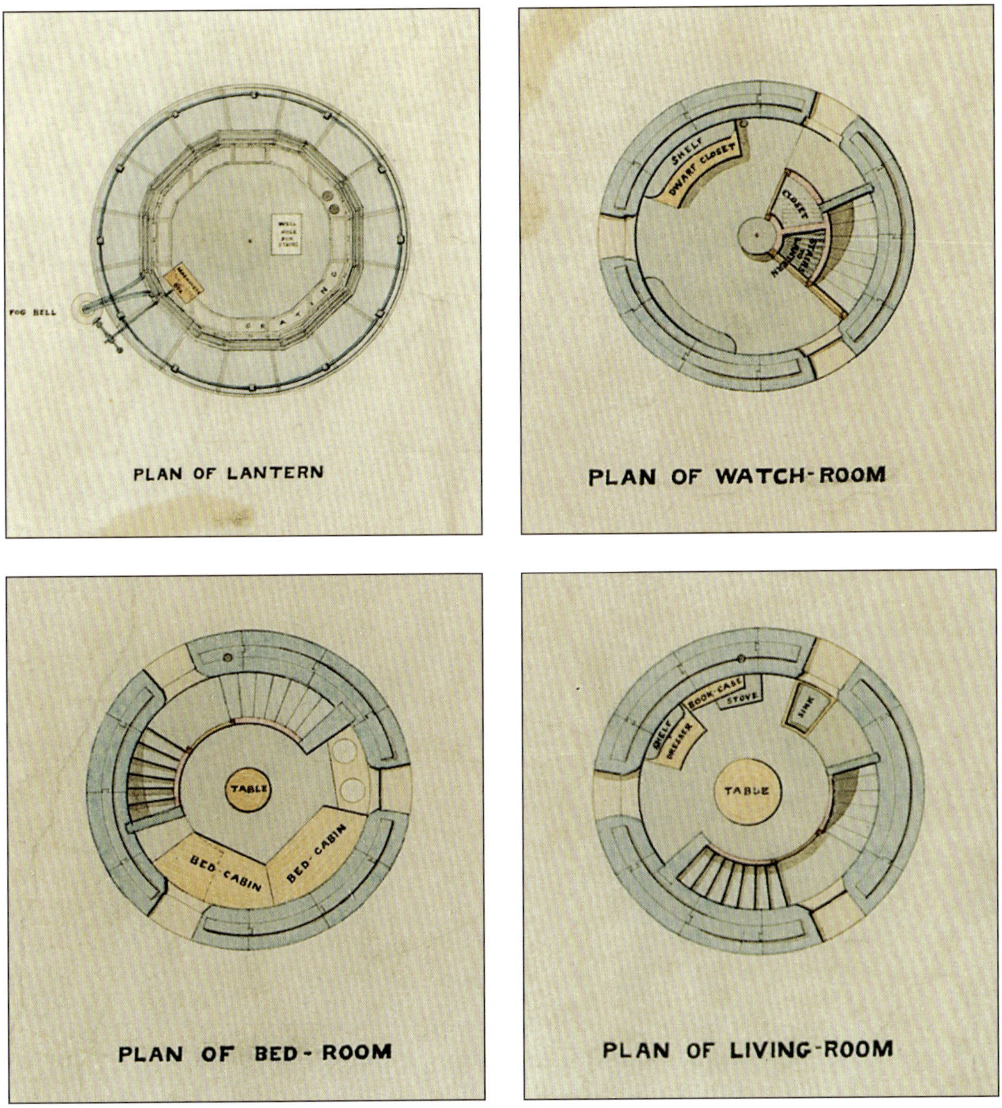

23. Highlights of the planned lay-outs for four of the the rooms of Les Hanois ligththouse as depicted in the 1862 drawing by Mathews, Burges and Cooper. These show the lantern, the watch room, the bedroom and the living room. (Trinity House)

blocks would be integrated both horizontally and vertically through a series of dovetail joints; in essence construction was a three dimensional jigsaw puzzle. The blocks, each weighing several tons, would be pinned and then bonded together by quick drying cement invented by Smeaton.

Thus Les Hanois was to become one of the strongest towers ever built – in essence one solid block with the stone weighing about 2,500 tons and capable of withstanding the worst of the elements. The method of construction was also to become standard for subsequent rock towers, including the current Eddystone lighthouse, built in 1882 by James Douglass who succeeded his father as Trinity House's Chief Engineer.

Construction and Support

The designing engineer, James Walker – engineer-in-chief to Trinity House – decided that the granite for Les Hanois should be imported from the Carsew quarries near Penryn in Cornwall and supplied in rough blocks by Messrs W and J Freeman. Their performance over the following two years left something to be desired, according to Trinity House records. In February 1861 Messrs Freeman were admonished for not supplying stone as promptly as required and were "urgently desired" to do so on pain of the enforcement of the contract. In June that year Messrs Freeman expressed regret that there had been delays. They pleaded in excuse "the extreme severity of the past winter". The last vessel had been discharged and another vessel was about to leave with sufficient stone to complete a further seven courses. A further 100 stones were ready for shipment and no expense or labour would be spared to meet Trinity House's wishes.

The location of the lighthouse and the method of construction had influenced the decision on the materials handling facilities. The records show that if La Mauve had been chosen as the site for the lighthouse, Trinity House would have considered using Portelet, the closest sheltered bay, as a building yard and trans-shipment base. The committee who had inspected Hanois reef in July 1859 reported that the bay was well adapted for the purpose inasmuch as a view of the rocks could be obtained from the land above it. (Indeed, that is where – many years later – wives of keepers would signal to their husbands on duty in the lighthouse.) The use of Portelet would have entailed not only the construction of the building yard but also a breakwater and connecting pier to berth and shelter boats and barges. That would have been expensive.

So, with Le Bisseau chosen as the lighthouse location, Trinity House

24. Les Hanois lighthouse resident engineer William Douglass as depicted in later life. He commanded the "unbounded confidence" of his working parties.
(Commissioners of Irish Lights)

25. Professor Michael Faraday, the discoverer of electro-magnetic induction, who as Scientific Adviser to Trinity House inspected the Hanois light before installation. He gave the light his "unqualified approbation". (The Royal Institution, London / Bridgeman Art Library)

adopted its alternative proposal – the use of a newly constructed pier at St Peter Port harbour. In a letter to the Bailiff, dated July 27th, 1859, Trinity House asked if it could use the new Castle Walk pier for laying out and dressing the stone needed for the lighthouse. The pier would be equipped with a shed, a crane and other handling equipment. The Corporation also asked if the vessels and barges employed in construction work could be allowed to arrive and depart "without payment of pier or any other dues".

The States agreed to these requests on the understanding that the permission would not extend beyond the end of the year 1862. The Bailiff assured Trinity House that should any unforeseen difficulties arise to prevent the completion of the lighthouse in the specified time, he would be prepared to lay before the States a request for an extension.

As was to be proved, it was a tight schedule, but the logistics worked well. The Cornish granite would arrive in smacks and be offloaded on to the quay. There craftsmen would dress and number the stones.

These finished stones would then be carried by barge along the south coast of Guernsey to Le Bisseau. There a crane was installed on the almost flat eastern side of the rock to lift the stones on to rail-borne trucks. This little railway ran for about 50 yards to the tower construction site where a large central crane was erected.

Gangs of up to 16 men were employed at the construction site at any one time. Permission was granted by the War Department for the men to use barracks at Rocquaine Castle, then said to be empty and of "no use" (the building is now the Fort Grey Shipwreck Museum). During the latter period of construction the men were employed building the lighthouse keepers' cottages at Portelet when the weather was too bad to work offshore.

Trinity House records show that the spiritual welfare of these gangs were not overlooked for at the end of the construction period the Revd Charles Guille of St Peter Port Town Church thanked the Corporation for their contribution of £20 towards the enlargement of a room in which he had performed "Divine Service for the Stranger Workmen". The Revd Guille was curate at the church between 1859 and 1869. His father, the Very Revd William Guille was Dean of Guernsey and rector of the same church.

The Light

The other major decision to be taken concerned the all-important light, and here there was surprising controversy. In March 1861 it was resolved that Les Hanois should have a red revolving light of the first order. It was later resolved that there would also be a fog bell with "striking machinery". So far, so good.

The ensuing row – between Trinity House and the Board of Trade – concerned the manufacturer and supplier of the lighting apparatus. The Corporation wanted the Midlands-based Chance Brothers and were happy to accept their tender bid.

It seemed a safe choice. Chance Brothers, which had established their lighthouse factory at Smethwick, Birmingham, in 1848, had earned themselves a reputation as the leading suppliers of optical apparatus in Britain. By the middle of the 19th century virtually all glass prisms or specialist lighthouse optics were being supplied by either French manufacturers or Chance Brothers. Near the end of the 19th century Chance would be supplying much of the world's lighthouse optical equipment.

Nevertheless, the Board of Trade made it plain that it could not concur with Trinity House's acceptance of Chance Brothers' tender. It wanted to see other manufacturers being invited to compete.

The argument went on and in July 1862 – only a few months from the November 1st first light exhibition deadline – the Board of Trade dug in its heels. A Trinity House minute shows that "their Lordships do not find from our Letters any ground for regarding the Case of the Apparatus in question, as one of a peculiar or exceptional Work, and therefore feel that they would not be justified in sanctioning a Departure from the established principle, and must repeat their request that Tenders for the Apparatus may be obtained from the Makers usually invited in such cases".

But time was running out. The Court of Trinity House wrote back that it had been communicating with Messrs Chance for some time; that their work was considered to be of an "exceptional character"; and that an arrangement had been entered into that would "render it very inconvenient" to postpone for other tenders to be invited. Furthermore, an unavoidable delay would arise from Chance Brothers' work being abandoned so that the exhibition of the Hanois light would not be achieved by that autumn.

The Board of Trade relented and on October 11th Trinity House received confirmation that Chance Brothers had indeed done a good job. It came in a report from none other than Professor Michael Faraday, the

26. Granite blocks, originally destined to be used in Les Hanois lighthouse, recovered from the seabed at Les Tielles, on Guernsey's south coast. The stone, some 100 pieces, was discovered in the late 1960s and recovered in 1973. It is thought that a barge loaded with the granite sank while being taken from St Peter Port to the Hanois construction site. Unfortunately it has not been possible to positively identify the man in the archived photograph. (Carel Toms Collection, Priaulx Library, Guernsey)

discoverer of electro-magnetic induction. This discovery, above all others, led to widespread electricity generation, and the the modern society we know today.

But it was as Scientific Adviser to Trinity House, a post which he was to hold from 1836 to 1865 – that Prof Faraday was inspecting the Hanois light. He went to Birmingham to inspect the light "both by day and by night". He gave the light his "unqualified approbation". As the Corporation recorded: "... it consists of 672 pieces of glass, but the adjustment of all is perfect according to the foci given and that those pieces which act together in one Panel act as one piece of glass".

In the end the light did not shine that autumn 1862. "Boisterous" weather in October that year delayed work on the lighthouse, including the installation of the lighting apparatus.

The engineer in charge

The man chosen as resident engineer to oversee all this construction work was William Douglass, the younger son of Nicholas Douglass, the man who had suggested the lateral and vertical dovetailing of the granite blocks at Hanois. William was appointed in October 1859 – when he was just 28 years old – at a salary of £300 per annum.

This was his first major assignment. He had proved himself an able scholar in spite of his itinerant life accompanying his father to various lighthouse sites. As a teenager he was apprenticed to the engineering firm of Robert Stephenson and Company of Newcastle-on-Tyne. By all accounts he was a diligent apprentice, working from 6am to 7pm and then studying at home for the rest of the evening. And then in 1852 he was appointed by Trinity House to assist his father in building the Bishop Rock lighthouse in the Scilly Isles, taking over from his brother James.

William quickly demonstrated that he was an intrepid and talented engineer. Like his father he possessed iron nerve and tireless energy. He regularly accompanied working parties to the storm tossed construction site, usually being the first off the boat.

His biographer, Thomas Williams, said that wherever he worked, William Douglass commanded the "unbounded confidence" of his working parties... "his courage and resources being equal to every emergency". An engineer who worked closely with Douglass – confusingly, a Mr William Williams – testified to the "heroic qualities" displayed by his chief.

William Douglass, then, was to prove an inspired and inspiring choice as the resident engineer for Les Hanois.

CHAPTER SIX

HANOIS LIGHTHOUSE - THE TRUE "SAILORS' FRIEND"

As if to reinforce the urgency for the tower's construction a 221 – ton Belgian sailing ship, the *Constant* carrying timber for the Spanish government, was wrecked in "tempestuous" weather on Guernsey's south west coast. It was late on January 21st 1860 that the *Constant,* a schooner-galliot out of Ostend, found herself battling with the elements close to the island's reefs. On port tack and under close-reefed mainsail and topsail the vessel was driven by a heavy squall on to rocks in Rocquaine Bay.

Fortunately the crew of 13, commanded by Leopold Defrance, was able to use the ship's jolly boat to escape to shore. As the weather abated Belgium's Vice-Consul on the island, Mr F de Putron, hired a gang of 40 men to remove anchors and chains and other provisions and equipment from the stricken vessel.

Pro-lighthouse campaigners, including the local press, did not lose the opportunity to remind authorities that if there had been a warning light on the Hanois rocks the *Constant* would probably have been able to complete her voyage to Cartagena in Spain.

But there was already tangible evidence of progress. Three Trinity House barges and a tug had arrived in Guernsey by October the previous year. By March 1860 the first cargo of Cornish granite – some 20 blocks, each of three or four tons – had been shipped from Penryn to St Peter Port to be dressed on the Castle Walk worksite before being towed to Les Hanois. Two months later, on May 10th, the Commissioners of Lighthouses – led by Admiral Hamilton – visited Guernsey to inspect the lighthouse site.

Then, in August that year, came the grand stone-laying ceremony. In these days of media spin, when events are pre-announced, announced, and re-announced, it is interesting to see how the Guernsey media was kept in the dark about this important occasion. *The Comet* told readers on August

14th: “The memorial-stone of the Hanois Lighthouse will be formally laid tomorrow by the Bailiff. The ceremony will take place at 11 o’clock. The programme, if there be one, has not been communicated to the Press so that we cannot supply our readers with other particulars.”

In the event the ceremony was impressive and was watched by crowds of onlookers who had ventured out to the reef in a flotilla of boats. The Bailiff, Sir Peter Stafford Carey and his wife, accompanied by several Jurats from Guernsey’s Royal Court, sailed to Les Hanois in a Trinity House tug.

Sir Peter laid the foundation with “all masonic formula and solemnity”, according to *The Comet.* Its report continued that, level in hand, the Bailiff then addressed the assembled crowd:

“The first stone of the lighthouse is now laid. I may safely say that from the foundation of the world to the present day there never stood on this rock an assembly like the present. The occasion is worthy of our meeting. The sea, whose dark grey waves we now behold, overhung with clouds, is the great pathway of nations, over which is borne to some of the wealthiest capitals of Europe the commerce of the East and of the West.

“The perils that attend the navigation of these waters are brought feelingly home to us by the melancholy wrecks that are cast upon our shores, but it is not alone by the wrecks that are cast upon our shores that those perils are to be measured. Many a gallant vessel, full of life and hope, has gone down to the bottom with every soul on board, leaving nothing behind but, perhaps, some solitary spar floating on the waves to indicate its fate!

“It is to protect the mariner from these perils that this lighthouse is to be built – to warn him of the danger and to guide him on his way. We may be assured that in the construction of the building nothing that skill, science, and energy can effect will be wanting. And let us trust that when completed it will, with the blessing of Providence, realise the wishes of those by whom it is founded.”

The crowd then gave three cheers.

The next to speak was Jurat Henry Tupper, chairman of the States lighthouse committee and one of the most enthusiastic and persuasive

27. One of the many cartoons drawn by Hanois boatman Richard Tostevin. A caption would be superfluous. (R Tostevin)

advocates for the tower. This work would later be recognised by the French community in Guernsey who, in 1875, commissioned a fine granite model of Les Hanois lighthouse to be presented to Jurat Tupper. Unfortunately, he died before the presentation could be made. The Tupper family bequeathed the 4ft model to the Royal Court and it is now displayed appropriately in the Fort Grey Shipwreck Museum.

In his speech Jurat Tupper said that value of good lights on dangerous shores were now admitted by all. England, France and the United States of America were among countries erecting improved lighthouses and "marking their progress in civilisation".

Guernsey, he said, was indebted to Trinity House for having ordered the erection of the lighthouse which would not only be beneficial in the preservation of life and property but also to the general trade of the Channel. He hoped that the building work would be completed without accident (sadly, this was not to be) and when finished it would be a light reflecting the greatest credit on all who had conceived and executed the work.

Another three cheers were then called for – this time to celebrate Trinity House; William Douglass the resident engineer; Mr J Dixon, the Superintendent of Works; and the men employed on the works. It is recorded the cheers were given heartily.

The official party then partook of a "plentiful supply" of champagne and refreshment provided by Mr Douglass before returning to Portelet at 2pm. Mr Douglass then dined with members of the Royal Court at Durman's Hotel.

It was intended that the lighthouse would take two years to build but, as already indicated, bad weather delayed progress. For the men working on the reef, it could be a hazardous occupation. There would always be someone on watch for rogue seas and if Le Bisseau looked like being swamped the men would jump into a stand-by boat and row to safety.

On one occasion, five men were swept off the rock and half drowned. One died six weeks later while another is reported to have "lost his reason". In October 1860 there was a narrow escape when a Trinity House boat carrying four men capsized in the heavy seas running off the Hanois rocks. "We are glad to say, nothing more serious than their immersion and exposure to peril resulted from the accident," wrote *The Comet*.

In the same month of 1862, when the light should have been shining, a prolonged gale prevented the relief of one of the gangs. There was widespread concern for the men for they were running short of food. The men had flown a warning flag to advise those on shore of their plight. William Douglass himself earned praise for action taken during this incident.

There were plans for towing the island's lifeboat, the *Rescuer,* overland from St Sampson's to Rocquaine to assist in the rescue but fortunately – thanks to William Douglass – it was not needed. He secured the services of a large Rocquaine fishing boat and joined the fishermen in taking out essential provisions to the stranded men. It is recorded that the sea was rolling and breaking heavily and the fishing boat had to carry a large amount of canvas to reach Le Bisseau. Casks of food and drink were thrown overboard and hauled in by the grateful workmen. Conditions were difficult: rough seas, a stiff breeze and poor visibility. Major General Marcus John Slade, the Lieutenant Governor, later drew the attention of Trinity House Elder Brethren to Douglass's praiseworthy "energy" in visiting Les Hanois in such heavy seas.

In another incident a cargo of dressed granite was lost off Les Tielles, on the island's south coast, presumably as it was being taken from St Peter Port to Les Hanois. The stone – some 100 pieces, mostly four feet long – was discovered in the late 1960s by diver Len Mechem and recovered in 1973 by a local trawler, the *Malamok*. Writing in the *Guernsey Evening Press and Star* author and journalist Carel Toms surmised that a barge loaded with the granite had been lost off Les Tielles, near Le Creux Mahie. Geologist Dr R A Roach studied the stone and confirmed that it had indeed come from Cornwall rather than Guernsey. Carel Toms added that the valuable grey stone was "now finding its way into buildings all over the island".

In spite of these set backs and, at times, the appalling conditions, steady progress was made in the tower's construction. And as the structure rose, so the interest of the general public seemed to grow. Boat excursions to the Hanois reef became a new attraction for locals and tourists alike.

The popularity of such trips can be gauged from a report in *The Comet* of June 27th, 1861:

"A scene most enlivening was presented last Monday evening at the landing pier, where many hundreds of persons congregated to witness the departure of excursions for the vicinage of the Hanois rocks, on one of which is a lighthouse now in course of erection, on the south-west coast of Guernsey. Two trips thither were made by the Cygnus, one of the vessels of the Weymouth and Channel Islands' Steampacket Company. On both occasions her decks were stowed with a compact mass, nearly 800 individuals, chiefly of the operative class, having availed themselves of the first opportunity which had yet offered for visiting a spot destined to become famous in nautical annals and render great service in the cause of humanity."

By March 1862 the workmen had raised the stonework to a height of about 60 feet. A further 12 feet of stonework – dressed and numbered – was stacked in the St Peter Port harbour work yard waiting to be trans-shipped and fitted. "So noiselessly are operations being carried on at the Hanois, westward of Guernsey, that seldom is anything said about the lighthouse," reported *The Comet*. "The workmanship is exquisite and the manner in which the whole is framed and dovetailed together must ensure perfect solidity."

But still shipwrecks were occurring, as if to emphasise the need for the light's completion. *Globe,* a 179 tons schooner-brig from Jersey, struck the

Hanois reef or possibly other rocks west of Lihou, on April 6th, 1862, after her Master – a Captain Austin – had made navigational errors in appalling weather conditions.

The ship was in ballast on a voyage from Jersey to Boston but after 57 days at sea, battered and disabled by heavy gales, she put back for her home port. At about 3 am the vessel was driven on to rocks that Captain Austin mistakenly took to be Roches Douvres, some 20 miles south of Guernsey. Fortunately the crew of seven managed to take the ship's boat and landed at Vazon Bay on Guernsey's west coast later that morning. Guernsey pilots saw the *Globe* sink north west of L'Ancresse Bay to the north of Guernsey. The editorial generated by the incident was familiar. "Thus this accident may again be put down to the absence of a light on these dangerous rocks," commented *The Star.*

28. The old harbour, St Peter Port, Guernsey, in 1865. (Carel Toms Collection, Priaulx Library, Guernsey)

Good progress on the lighthouse construction was made that summer and early in July a committee from Trinity House travelled in the steamer *Vestal* to Guernsey to inspect the work and to deliver the lantern and other equipment. They found that the stonework had risen to the floor of the watch room.

The committee also accompanied William Douglass on a tour of inspection of the keepers' cottages, under construction at Portelet. They found that the dwellings were in a "forward state" and being built "in a substantial good manner". The committee also recommended that a flag staff should be erected on an adjacent hill to allow communication with the lighthouse.

By August 13th the last course of stone was reported to be in the hands of the workmen. Six days later, in his weekly report to the Court of Trinity House, James Walker stated that the lighthouse was ready to receive the lantern. Messrs Wilkins, the contractors, were instructed to take the "necessary steps" to install the equipment.

29. A view of the Albert Dock area of St Peter Port Harbour, Guernsey in the 1860s. The steamer Alert is seen alongside Albert Pier. (Carel Toms Collection, Priaulx Library, Guernsey)

In mid October the Trinity House steam tender *Argus* arrived in Guernsey, carrying the lens. The Elder Brethren of the Court were assured that the lighting apparatus had been safely landed at St Peter Port. Unfortunately "boisterous weather" held up the transfer of the precious lens and on October 27th Douglass was forced to admit that only a small portion of the apparatus had been landed on Le Bisseau. Consequently it would be "impracticable" to exhibit the light on or about November 1st as had been advertised.

Nevertheless, the weather relented and construction work rapidly moved to its climax so that on November 24th Douglass was able to report that the lighting apparatus was now "nearly all fitted up" and would be ready for the exhibition within a few days.

Five days later *Vestal* arrived in Guernsey with the first three Hanois keepers. The steamer also delivered oil and lighting stores to the lighthouse. The lantern machinery was demonstrated for the benefit of the visiting Trinity House committee and it was found to be very stiff. The committee ordered the machinery to be kept going daily, to bring it up to its proper revolution of 12 minutes. The light, it decreed, would be exhibited for two hours at sunset on the following Monday evening, December 1st, 1862.

Trinity House minutes record the events of that historic day:

"Monday December 1st – Fresh SW wind and fine. Got 20 tons of coal alongside at daylight. Called on General Slade, the Lt. Governor... 4.45pm Left the Harbour and proceeded for the Hanois and when clear of the land the Light opened about eight miles distant, showing an excellent red, the flashes were too quick, about 36 instead of 45 seconds, about eight seconds good light waning to about 25 seconds dark. At 6.20pm the Light extinguished."

The Les Hanois light was officially exhibited for the first time a week later, on 8th December watched by a small group from Trinity House led by the Deputy Master, Captain William Pigott. The Lieutenant Governor and Bailiff were invited to join the group but they were unable to, due to a previous engagement.

Vestal then left the Hanois reef. It was later recorded by Trinity House that "at 5.30 the Light bore SSE distant 3 miles, from whence the Light of the Lantern is seen clearly. Steered NEE ¼E making the Caskets at 6.10pm bearing ENE distant 13 miles, At 6.38 the Hanois Light dipped bearing SW ¾W, distant 13½ miles."

After all of the campaigning and controversies, and in marked contrast to the laying of the foundation stone, the shining of the first light seemed like an anticlimax. *The Comet,* whose editorials and news items about the lighthouse had featured so prominently over the previous decades, could manage only two lines. Under a sub-heading "Local Record" it reported: "The Hanois Light was kindled on Monday, and will be continued regularly henceforth."

However, the first light was marked, and in a most appropriate way. On December 20th a French brig, *L'Abondance* carrying wheat from Marseilles, put into Guernsey roadstead with its master declaring that but for the light the vessel would have been lost and in all probability with all hands. Given the combination of moonless nights and north westerly gales that was then occurring, he was sure that other vessels had also benefited.

Trinity House was told of the tribute by Capt N Le Messurier, described as the "late" Constable of St Peter Port, who had been informed by the brig's master that his vessel "would have been dashed to pieces on the West Coast" had it not been for "the timely warning of the true 'Sailor's Friend'".

Capt Le Messurier, a retired ship Master and examiner of Guernsey pilots, was probably described as the "late" Constable because shortly before he had been appointed the first Trinity House Agent for Hanois at an annual salary of £40. Another early appointment was that of Thomas Guillieme, an experienced pilot employed by Douglass during the construction work. Guillieme was appointed attendant boatman and required to "find a boat with seven men, visit twice a month, fill and take off water, coals, keepers, agents etc" for £53.11s.0d per annum. A further 20 shillings would be paid for each additional trip.

Douglass himself was rewarded for his work at Les Hanois. It had been a magnificent achievement – the construction of a trend-setting rock tower in the most difficult of conditions at a total cost of £25,296.

On January 9th 1863 the Board of Trade confirmed its approval to the transfer of Mr and Mrs Douglass from Les Hanois to the lighthouse construction works at Wolf Rock – midway between Land's End and the Scilly Isles – at an annual salary of £450; a 50 per cent increase.

Once again William Douglass was taking over from his brother. James Douglass had been appointed resident engineer at Wolf Rock but, on the death of James Walker in October 1862, he was promoted to be Trinity House chief engineer. As already indicated, William Douglass would again demonstrate not only his engineering skills but also his bravery. On a number of occasions he led his men through the surf breaking on the rock. One incident was reminiscent of his time at Hanois. Realising that a work party was running short of food and water, Douglass took charge of a boat and steered it to Wolf Rock "in the midst of the seething caldron, and with infinite coolness and skill".

William Douglass went on to become resident engineer for the construction of two lighthouses on the Great and Little Basses Reefs in Cyprus before being appointed chief engineer to the Commissioners of Irish Lights in 1878. During his 22 years in Ireland (he retired of ill health in 1900, aged 69) Douglass distinguished himself with many achievements, most notably the design and construction of the Fastnet Rock lighthouse, off the southern tip of the island.

But in 1863 there were still Hanois-related tasks to perform before Douglass could leave Guernsey.

First there was the matter of the work site at St Peter Port Harbour. Trinity House had agreed to reinstate the quay but in the end the States of Guernsey asked if the crane, buildings and equipment could be allowed to remain rather than be removed. Trinity House replied that the Elder Brethren would have "great pleasure" in transferring all of the buildings and equipment without charge to the Harbour Committee. An inventory of the work yard, prepared by Douglass, was appended. The letter from the Court of Trinity House, dated August 1st 1863, asked the Bailiff if he would "convey to the States of Guernsey the thanks of this Corporation for the courtesy which has been shewn to its members, and for the facilities afforded to its various officers during the progress of the work now finished".

The Bailiff, Sir Peter Stafford Carey, thanked the Elder Brethren for the "handsome manner" in which they had transferred the works and premises to the States. He added: "I shall also have great pleasure in conveying to the States, at their next meeting, the expression of the thanks of the Corporation, as communicated to me in your letter, and I am assured that it will be highly gratifying to the States to receive such an announcement."

The workmen's barracks at Fort Grey were vacated, cleaned and whitewashed. The Secretary of State for War, the Marquess of Hartington – later to become the Duke of Devonshire – was given Trinity House's "best thanks". In a quaint request, more akin to the handover of a rented flat, the Minister was "acquainted that the keys will be delivered up to any person he may see fit to appoint to receive them".

It is evident from the reports of visiting Trinity House inspection parties that work on the keepers' cottages was progressing less than satisfactorily. In May 1863 it was reported that "much delay seems to be taking place in regard to finishing. Painters were at work who said they expected to be finished by the end of the month".

In July, a month after the keepers and their families had moved in, it was found that the internal painting and distemper did not seem "very good" and that the establishment would need to be painted again the following year. The wood used for the stairs appeared not to have been well seasoned giving rise to a spring in the tread. Externally the dwellings were in "nice order" but the inspection party regretted that cement should have been placed over the stone, "destroying the effect and increasing the cost". It was also found that the toilets needed ventilation!

30. This handsome granite model of Les Hanois lighthouse was commissioned in 1875 by the French community in Guernsey, to recognise the work of Jurat Henry Tupper, chairman of the States lighthouse committee, who did so much in the campaign for the construction of the tower. Unfortunately he died before he was able to receive the model. It is now exhibited in the Fort Grey Shipwreck Museum in Guernsey. (Robbie Goldsmith)

There was also work to be completed in the lighthouse itself. In July 1863 – almost seven months after the exhibition of the first light – the lighthouse was "still full of workmen". It was reckoned that final commissioning would take a further two months at least.

While, the lantern and lighting apparatus were found to be in good order the fog bell machinery was causing a problem. The inspecting committee found that the machinery had been set to strike four blows a minute but this was not quite frequent enough to retain the sound. Consequently the revolution was set at seven blows per minute.

The Trinity House inspectors tested the bell as they left the lighthouse. They found that the sound was not very good, even though the wind was in their favour. This seemed to confirm the experience of the accompanying pilot who said that on one occasion when he was in his boat at Grand Hanois rock the bell was inaudible although at Pleinmont Head, three or four times the distance from the lighthouse, the bell could be heard plainly. "The bearings of the two positions not diverging very much, the cause must be sought in some of the caprices sound appears to indulge in," records the Trinity House minute.

In the tradition of Trinity House there were to be many subsequent inspections, and invariably the reports were favourable: such as "in most excellent order" – May 1868; "all in good order" – May 1869 and May 1870; and "in very good and efficient order" – June 1874.

Over the decades the storm battered landing stage and steps would need to be repaired from time to time. As we will see, the equipment and accommodation would be modernised. A helipad would be fitted to the top of the lighthouse. But the basic granite structure would remain unchanged and seemingly impregnable – a tribute to its designers and builders.

To quote again from Victor Hugo's "Toilers of the Sea": "The destroyer in ambush now bears a lighted torch in his hand".

CHAPTER SEVEN
TOWER OF STRENGTH

Lighthouse keepers were a special breed. Self-reliant and resourceful, content with their own company, they knew that the weeks spent on duty in the rock tower (or "tower rock station" in the parlance of keepers) would be ruled by the clock and governed by routine. Shift patterns and duties were rigorously observed. But there was also plenty of free time – for relaxation, reflection, exercise and hobbies. As we will see, some keepers could be particularly creative – even obsessive – in the way they followed these pursuits.

But first, it might be useful to visualise the layout of their vertical home-cum-workspace. The interior design of Les Hanois is typical of 19th century rock towers although it is somewhat smaller and narrower than some.

There are, in essence, seven rooms in the tower, the main ones being about 13 feet in diameter and nine feet high. Illustrations of the original design clearly show the neatness of the arrangement. The entrance doorway and passage was constructed above the water tank. Climbing the granite steps, lighthouse keepers in the 1860s would have passed through the water room, the oil room, the store room, the living room, the bedroom, the watch room and then into the handsome lantern.

Modernisation at various times brought about a number of changes in the use of some of the lower rooms and, as we will see, the lantern gallery was remodelled in the later years of manned operation. But essentially, the lighthouse today is structurally the tower constructed at the beginning of the early 1860s.

A keeper arriving by boat was faced with a climb up steps even before he entered the lighthouse for, depending on the state of the tide, there could be as many as 30 slippery steps to negotiate before he reached the landing stage at the foot of the tower. And then there were seven iron rungs to climb before the entrance door of the lighthouse was reached.

The entrance door leads into a tunnel-like passage. The steps leading up are a magnificent sight, as retired Principal Keeper Norman Wakley recalls: "It is lovely to see... from the base of the tower the stone steps looked like an open pack of cards. The finishing is wonderful; the ends of the steps are rounded off – just like a carpet of stone. They are fitted so well that the steps look like a stone pole from floor to ceiling."

The lowest rooms were used to store fuel, oil and provisions. After the old coal fired cooking range in the kitchen had been replaced with more modern appliances the old coal store was converted into a shower room. "The shower was a real luxury for before that all we had for washing was a basin in the kitchen," said Norman Wakley. The shower room backs on to the lavatory, another apparent luxury. "The toilet was another thing that Hanois had that many other towers didn't have. In those places you had to use a bucket ... and make sure you knew which way the wind was blowing when you emptied it!"

Gerry Douglas-Sherwood also has vivid memories of that toilet from his days in Hanois as a Supernumerary Assistant Keeper in the early 1970s. "It was dark and damp and often crawling with sea slaters," he wrote in the Trinity House periodical *Lamp*. The toilet was flushed with sea water and periodically pumped into a storage tank beside the coal bunker. "To do this a remote electric pump would be taken across the landing and thrown into the sea. The person assigned to watch the water level in the storage tank had the task of climbing across the coal with a flashlight and peering into the tank, being ready to holler 'Stop' once the water level reached the required height. The urgency was minimised by the fact the pump's delivery rate was painfully slow." Douglas-Sherwood added, perhaps superfluously: "Less demanding calls of nature were accommodated by an enamel saucepan on the window sill outside the bedroom door."

Going up the stairs, the first real room you come to is the winch room (the original oil room). A manual winch, situated in the centre of this room, was used to hoist provisions, fuel and water up through a doorway.

The next room up the tower was once used as a food store and magazine. It was here that explosive charges and detonators for the old fog signal were kept prior to installation of an electric fog signal emitter. In later years this storeroom was converted into an engine room with two

31. The winch room/oil room in Les Hanois lighthouse, as it was in the early 1970s. (Association of Lighthouse Keepers)

32. The service room at Les Hanois in the period 1973-75 with its control panels for all three engines, a Pye "Hamble" radio telephony set, a coastal chart and the monthly and annual station journals. (Association of Lighthouse Keepers)

Lister diesel-driven generators. Keepers remark that given all the equipment crammed into the small room, it was not easy to move about. It was not unusual for the engine nearest the door to be inadvertently shut down as a keeper knocked the cut out device as he squeezed past to reach the rear engine.

Next on the ascent is the hub of the lighthouse – the kitchen-cum-living room. There is a sink by one of the two storm shuttered windows, chairs, storage cupboards, a radio and television. For much of its life this room was equipped with a Rayburn coal-fired range that was used for cooking and heating. After the war this was replaced by a Hamco oil-fired range which in turn, in the final years of the tower's occupation, was replaced with an electric cooker, electric fire and a microwave oven.

All fresh water had to be delivered and kept in a 2,000-gallon tank at the base of the tower. On at least one occasion this water became accidentally contaminated with oil when the diesel feed was wrongly attached to the water inlet (there were also occasions when water contaminated the diesel tanks). A job lot of paper kitchen towels were brought from shore to mop the oil from the top of the water tank.

Water was naturally regarded as a precious resource, as Harold Taylor, Principal Keeper in the 1970s, related in the Yourmemories.co.uk website. "We had to make most water serve several purposes. For example, the hot water from the vegetable cooking would be kept to swill off the greasy plates or cooking utensils. Then the washing up water would be kept for wiping over the floor. Very little water was put down the sink, especially greasy water. The waste pipe was of lead, and quite large in diameter, but it sagged between the supports and grease very quickly congealed and could cause a blockage.

"Most water was tipped into a slop bucket and either carried down the steps to be cast into the sea, or cast from a doorway into a passing sea at high water. The landing was awash then except on neap tides. From plugged holes in the waste pipe it could be seen that on many occasions neglect had arisen that had caused difficulties."

Boatman Richard Tostevin well remembers such a 'difficulty': "I recall a time in the 1990s when there was a serious blockage in the tower's drain. Trinity House sent out two guys from Cornwall to unblock the drain. It must have been really blocked for these guys spent five weeks trying to sort out the problem. Eventually they dug a hole at the bottom of the tower. Both men were in this hole when they managed to clear the blockage. You can imagine the state they were in... 80 feet of pressure bearing down. They were well covered. It was not pleasant."

It was not only the plumbing that could pose domestic problems. Paul Davis, Assistant Keeper in the 1980s, has memories of the oil-fired range. "It was temperamental and we often had problems of 'blow back'. But there was always a large kettle kept hot on the range for a ready supply of tea."

Maintaining the pattern of normal domestic life, keepers climbed the stairs from the living area to the bedroom. Originally this room was equipped with the traditional banana-shaped wooden bunks, built into the side of the tower. A small table was placed in the centre of the room. Keepers returning after the German occupation during the 1939-45 war found that the bunks had been replaced by utilitarian rectangular metal-framed beds. These took up much more of the available space. The reason for the change in sleeping arrangements is unclear. It is possible that the German occupiers replaced the unfamiliar bunks. There are also reports that a visiting mechanic re-establishing the light and other equipment after the war reported an insect infestation of the wooden panelling and bunks which then had to be stripped out.

Next up the stairs is the service or watch room containing the control panels for the lighthouse's three engines, battery charging units and the radio transmitters. Radio tests were carried out two or three times a day, either with a coastal radio station, a coastguard station, or among a group of lighthouses and light vessels within range. Hanois was in the Nab Tower group which also included Casquets, Shambles light vessel, Owers light vessel, Royal Sovereign light vessel and Royal Sovereign Tower. The working frequency was 1662 Khz while the calling frequency was 2182 Khz.

The service room was also equipped with an Admiralty chart showing the immediate coastal area. It was here that the station's journals were filled in daily.

The next and final stage of the annular staircase results in a disappointment for a visitor to Hanois. Originally the stairs would have led into the impressive lantern, but today – as was the case in the final decades of manned operation – it provides the entrance to another engine room. This upper engine room contains the third diesel engine, compressors for the fog signal, and a series of alkaline batteries.

A vertical metal ladder leads to the beautiful lens set, at shoulder height, on a meticulously maintained roller base. When *Guernsey Weekly*

THE NEW LIGHT-TOWER AT ST. PIERRE-PORT, GUERNSEY.

33. The "new" light tower at St Peter Port Harbour, Guernsey, as depicted in the Illustrated London News on March 30th, 1867. The tower – built shortly after the lighthouse at Les Hanois – stands at the end of a breakwater extending from Castle Cornet that forms the south arm of St Peter Port Harbour. The pier-head light tower was commissioned on March 1st 1867. The Illustrated London News described it as a "handsome granite structure", furnished with a third-class dioptric lens, the light of which was 50 feet above high water at average spring tides. The light could be seen at a distance of nine miles (today its range is 16 miles). The light tower was designed by Peter Le Lièvre, a member of the Harbour Committee chaired by Sir Peter Stafford Carey, the Bailiff who had played such a prominent role in the campaign for Les Hanois lighthouse. (Illustrated London News)

Press reporter Ian Yeaman visited the tower in December 1962 – exactly 100 years after the first Hanois light had shone – he noticed the brass plate which read: "First order dioptric holophotal revolving light, manufactured by Chance Brothers and Co., Glassworks, Birmingham 1862." Dioptric or refracting apparatus is accredited to Augustin Fresnel, a Frenchman. The system directs the rays of a light source into a beam by means of lenses and prisms. Holophotal is a quaint description for an apparatus making available all the light of a lamp. Dioptric lights are classified according to strength which is dependent on the focal plane. In 1862 there were six "orders", the first being the strongest with a focal distance of 920mm.

34. The fourth order lens of Les Hanois, photographed in May 1993. (Association of Lighthouse Keepers)

35. The Hanois lighthouse kitchen, as it was in the 1973-75 period, with a Hamco oil-fired range, a sink with three plastic bowls (one for personal washing, another for clothes washing and the other general washing), and a black and white television set. (Association of Lighthouse Keepers)

The original lens had 16 faces and in the first years of operation shone a revolving red light. A navigation chart for 1862 described the character thus: a revolving red light flashing every 45 seconds from a height of 100 feet and visible for 16 miles. Over the years the character of the light changed several times. Currently the Hanois signals two white flashes every 13 seconds from a height of 33 metres. The present range is 20 miles.

In 1964 the lighthouse was completely modernised and converted from oil to diesel-generated electricity power. The station was stripped of all equipment, including the original lantern and lens. A new, smaller lantern was prefabricated at Trinity House's Blackwall workshops. The light was reduced in intensity with a lens of fourth order.

The old explosive fog signal and fog bell were replaced by a compressed air Supertyfon fog signal. Today the lighthouse is equipped with a modern electric emitter fog signal installed between the solar panels on the west side of the lighthouse.

But it was the previous fog warning system that provided the real colour and drama. There were, in fact, two warning systems – a large bell and an explosive warning device. The bell was controlled by a clock mechanism and, in foggy conditions, struck once every minute.

The explosive fog signal sounded every two-and-a-half minutes and was a much more exciting affair, especially with so much glass around. Again, Harold Taylor describes the operation:

"There was a huge arm that was wound down to hang the explosives on. Then this was wound up to be above the lantern roof for the charge to be exploded. The lantern was about 20 feet high, and the pivot of the arm was at gutter level, at least 16 feet up. A vertical rod came down from this pivot point which was controlled by a worm gear. The bottom end of the rod had a winding handle. One wound the handle and brought the jib down to waist level.

"When the jib was in the down position the ends of this bow piece was opposite two openable ports. In theory one put one's hands through the ports and suspended the quarter pound Tonite charges by their detonator on clips of the bow. When this was done the handle was wound and the jib described a large arc until it was vertical above the lantern roof. All this time there was a time clock ticking away, and at the prescribed time a bell would ring, so that you would then press the plunger and detonate the explosive."

But this was not all. Associated with the fog warning devices was the "fog clock", a type of barograph which when set in motion recorded on graph paper the time when the fog signals were sounding. Keepers needed this recorded evidence to claim inconvenience pay at the end of the month. In the 1970s stations sounding a bell only were awarded one (old) penny per hour while stations with explosives or compressed air devices received 2d an hour.

Inevitably, the system was open to abuse by some less scrupulous keepers who were anxious to boost their far from generous pay a little. This scam, as Taylor explained, was known as the "silent fog". The fog clock worked on the basis of vibrations making blips on the ink line running across the graph paper. Consequently, you could activate the machine – for instance, by banging a table – even if the fog signals were not sounding. "It could be very time consuming and not worth the effort, but when you consider that there was little to pass your time at anyway, what was more profitable than to take a book to the lantern and nudge the clock every time the bell rang?"

Appropriately, the lantern used to be the pinnacle of the lighthouse – surmounted by a weathervane – but in the summer of 1979 a helideck was installed on top. The 27ft diameter helicopter pad undoubtedly made it easier to transport people, equipment and supplies to and from the tower for the original helipad, at the base of the tower, was covered by the tides for much of the day and often remained slimy and slippery during the "dry" periods. However, the new helideck completely changed the aesthetic character of the tower. Les Hanois lighthouse now had an umbrella.

The helideck, stressed to take a load of just over 6,000 pounds, is reached by means of an iron rung ladder and trapdoors installed in the roof of the lantern gallery.

This, then, is the "estate agents'" view of Les Hanois Lighthouse, described by boatman Richard Tostevin as "the finest building in Guernsey". It is indeed a tower of strength, comprising 24,645 cubic feet of best quality Cornish granite dovetailed together in that innovative way introduced for the first time at Hanois.

But the spirit of Hanois comes from the people who worked there.

CHAPTER EIGHT

LIFE IN LES HANOIS: VIGILANCE, ROUTINE AND LEISURE

Life in a lighthouse was prescribed by the clock, whether it be the precise mechanism that dictated the character of the light or the rota that influenced the work, rest and relaxation of the keepers.

Following the introduction of "double manning" in 1974 keepers spent one month on duty in the lighthouse and one month off. While on duty the keepers' routine was dictated by the watch keeping times, typically: Middle watch (midnight to 4am), morning watch (4am to noon), afternoon watch (noon to 8pm), and evening watch (8pm to midnight). In three-handed rock towers, like Les Hanois, the afternoon duty might be split into two four-hour watches.

Another watch keeping pattern – this time with five watches – is illustrated below. Whatever routine was adopted, it had to be approved by Trinity House's District Superintendent.

Watch keeping arrangements for three-handed rock station (keepers A, B and C) (1951)

Seven day roster

0000 – 0400	A	C	B	A	C	B	A
0400 – 0800	B	A	C	B	A	C	B
0800 – 1600	C	B	A	C	B	A	C
1600 – 2000	A	C	B	A	C	B	A
2000 – 2400	B	A	C	B	A	C	B

Source: Trinity House

Paul Davis, Assistant Keeper at Les Hanois between 1984 and 1988, and again in 1995, recalls the system of communal cooking that was adopted by keepers when he was in the lighthouse: "Each keeper provided his own meat but it was the morning watchman – on duty from 4am to noon – who cooked the communal lunch. After lunch he went to bed, because he would be back on duty again at 8pm, and the afternoon watchman and 'day off' keeper would wash up."

It seems that such kitchen duties led to confusion and embarrassment from time to time, as Assistant Keeper Barry Hawkins remembers: "I once cooked and ate for lunch some of Alan Laing's meat ration by mistake." It was perhaps at such mealtimes that the individual traits of keepers became most apparent. Some followed peculiar diets. Varying degrees of personal hygiene, cleanliness and tidiness could be a source of inevitable irritation and, at times tension. At least one Hanois keeper earned the epithet "Piggy".

Of course, the keepers were not at Les Hanois for a social gathering. They were there to work, to keep the lighthouse in good working order. And during their tours of duty there were many duties to perform, some of which are illustrated by the following morning watch routine recorded during his days at Les Hanois by Gerry Douglas-Sherwood, now Archivist and one of the founders of the Association of Lighthouse Keepers.

Lighthouse Keepers' Duties

Morning Watch Routine (1970s)*

Every Morning — Clean engine and engine room floor; empty ashes and clean stove; wash kitchen floor; sweep and dust service room and lantern; fill coal buckets.

****

Monday — Top up batteries with distilled water and wipe battery tops; dust lens and ledges in lantern.

Tuesday — Sweep down stairs and clean windows.

Wednesday	Clean inside of oven and wash tea cloths and oven cloths.
Thursday	Sweep and dust bedroom; wipe down paintwork on stairs.
Friday	Check and top up batteries with distilled water if needed; wipe battery tops; wash out toilet; wash base of tower from the refrigerator down to the entrance.
Saturday	Wash down tower steps.
Note:	*Call out at 10.00 am except Sundays. Work after 10.00 am to prevent undue noise or as required by the Keeper in Charge or Principal Keeper.*

****

** The above is a typical day-to-day morning watch routine for keeping the tower and quarters clean on a rock station. The pattern was taken from the one followed at Les Hanois as recorded by Gerry Douglas-Sherwood of the Association of Lighthouse Keepers who served in the lighthouse in the early 1970s.*

In addition to these routine upkeep operations, keepers were also called upon to maintain the appearance and integrity of the lighthouse structure. That included painting or applying coats of lime.

Assistant Keeper Alan Laing – the officer who had his meat filched by Barry Hawkins – says that "Hanois was not a difficult station as far as work was concerned," but the task he did not enjoy was liming the landing and steps.

"I always took my turn until after about three years there when I had an asthma attack – lime dust blew about in the wind and it was impossible to keep it out of your lungs. Safety gear was either useless or impracticable. I ended up agreeing with my colleagues that I would do other tasks while they completed the liming."

Gerry Douglas-Sherwood points out that the tower had to be painted annually "and it was an accepted part of the keepers' duty to apply the paint". In his day there was no helideck on top of the lighthouse. "I took a brush to the top engine room exterior which is, if you can visualise the Hanois, like a large metal drum pierced with portholes surmounted with a lightship lantern – a unique combination. The views along the coastline of Guernsey could be quite breathtaking, and the sea around the tower was crawling with spider crabs and ormers (abalone), many of which found their way into the pot."

Indeed crabbing and fishing was one of the favourite free-time activities of the Hanois keepers. And many went about this hobby in an ingenious fashion.

36. Principal Keeper Robbie Goldsmith, photographed through the Hanois lantern, as he makes one of his many radio calls. (Robbie Goldsmith)

In 1951 the *Guernsey Star* reported that when conditions permitted Assistant Keepers Tom Whiston and Simon Reynolds fished with kites from the lighthouse gallery to keep themselves supplied with fresh fish. The late Freddie Robert, a quiet, retiring Principal Keeper, who served in Les Hanois in the late 1940s, is also credited with having fished from the tower, using a kite. In this way he and other "kite fishermen" were able to cast their fishing lines beyond the rocks that surround the tower. Boatman Richard Tostevin remembers the stories of this unusual fishing technique. "It could certainly be done, given the right wind," said Tostevin, who has spent a lifetime fishing, diving and abalone sea farming in Guernsey. "Mind you, it could not have been all that successful otherwise they would all have been doing it."

Tostevin once caught a large porbeagle shark near the base of the tower. "It must have weighed three hundredweight. I couldn't pull it in on my own so I had to call out and ask a couple of keepers to come down and help. I remember I sold the fish to a Chinese restaurant."

But it was the abundance of crabs that was the real Hanois attraction. Jack Daniels, an Assistant Hanois Keeper in the 1970s, pays tribute to Principal Keeper Norman Wakley as the master crabber. "Norman made his own crab pots while on leave. He used to stand on the landing stage and toss the pots over the rocks into the sea – no mean feat. Norman was a big, hefty guy... I doubt if anyone else could have done that. The pots were secured by rope tied to the boat mooring ring at the bottom of the tower. We had loads of crabs and occasionally the odd lobster."

He fondly remembers finding "huge crabs among the rocks". "We used to have lovely crab salads! There are two holes in the rocks called the letter boxes. We used to find the big crabs there. If they weren't there we used to put in some little crabs. For some reason the big ones would then appear and cover these little crabs as if to protect them."

Wakley also remembers catching conger eels off Hanois. "I once read a book that said the conger was a fish impossible to eat. We used to make some nice fish cakes. The congers were also baked. We used to take the back bone out and smear the inside with mustard. We would then fill it with stuffing. Lovely!"

The Hanois keepers passed their free time in a wide variety of ways. Many whiled away their periods of relaxation by reading, watching television, and chatting. Naturally, some were more communicative than others. Paul Davis was one of the keepers attributed with a ready wit. One day, in the mid 1980s, a trio of keepers were chatting when, as often happened, the question of sex cropped up. Principal Keeper Bert Tromans joked that he hadn't had a "hard on" since 1954. Paul pointed to the clock and quipped: "That's not bad Bert. It's only just turned 19.59."

During warm weather swimming and sunbathing were popular pursuits as the keepers took advantage of the lighthouse's location, perched on commodious rocks.

Wakley enthused again: “Hanois was lovely in the summer, especially in good weather when you could get outside and get some fresh air. Immediately to the south of the tower there is a rock which we call ‘Victoria’ because it looks like the statue. Between the tower and Victoria there is a pool which we called the ‘Lagoon’. This was a great place for swimming; so tempting in warm weather.”

Like a number of keepers, Robbie Goldsmith liked to take advantage of the lighthouse’s remoteness by sunbathing in the nude. One day, while topping up his tan lying on the helipad he found the wind was getting a bit too strong for comfort so he went to find more shelter down on the rocks by the ‘Lagoon’. “I was lying there, enjoying the sunshine, when I had a peculiar feeling that someone was watching me. I looked around and saw a seal laying there, watching me. I stared back at the seal because, frankly, I did not like the way it was looking at me! The seal then slipped into the water and swam away.”

But there was an unusual sequel to this story. A couple of days later his wife-to-be Joy was walking by Pezeries Point, overlooking the Hanois, when she thought she saw ‘a rock move’. It was a seal that appeared to be in distress, so Joy contacted the local animal shelter. “I was later told that the seal was heavily pregnant which prompted me to ask Robbie how close he had come to the animal.”

Many keepers were also interested in the bird life that frequented rock towers. Alan Laing was Keeper in Charge during one summer’s day in the early 1990s when relief keeper Roly Parsley became excited about the sighting of a particularly unusual visitor; a ‘big white bird’. It was in fact a snowy owl. Alan thought it might be an ‘escapee’ from a local zoo so he immediately telephoned Guernsey police. No-one claimed the poor bird which was being mobbed and tormented by gulls, much to the distress of bird watchers who by then had assembled on the nearby shoreline. Eventually, the owl realised that there were more conducive places to be than Les Hanois and it flew away.

Inevitably in the last decades of manned operation, television provided many of the keepers with their main means of spare time entertainment and relaxation. Alan Laing was one of those who was not mesmerised by the ‘box’. “I got really fed up with the television there as it never seemed to be off,” he recalls. “I like to read and the year before I got to Hanois I had started an Open University course so most of the time I had on my own was spent in reading and studying." He was eventually awarded a BA(Hons) degree in politics and economics.

Some Hanois keepers were notable artists, among them Desmond "Des" Sythes, an Assistant Keeper in the 1960s. Bearded Des exhibited a number of his paintings in the tower during his tour of duty. These included a thoughtful study of an old man and a view of boats moored at St Peter Port.

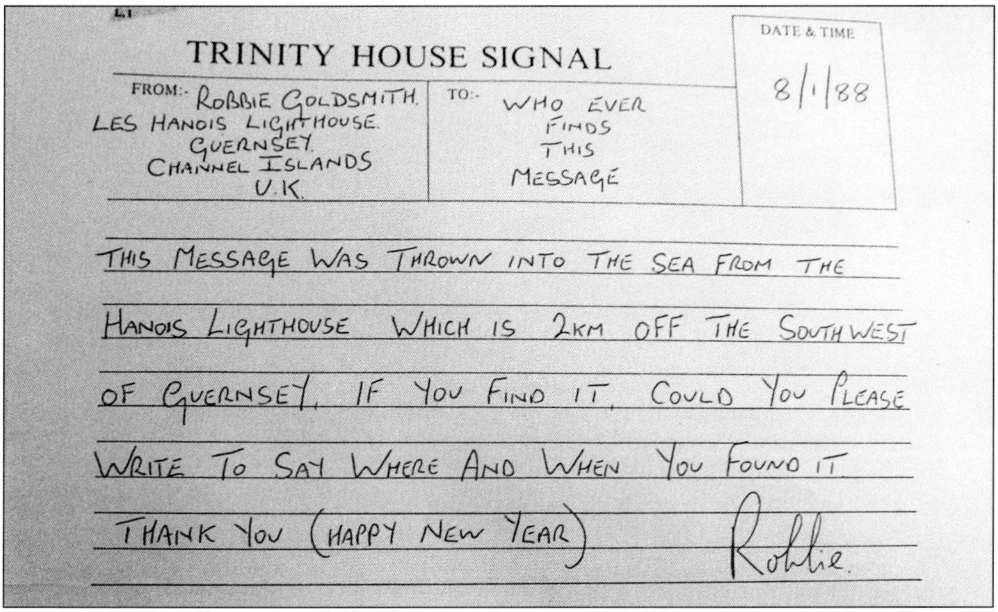

TRINITY HOUSE SIGNAL

DATE & TIME: 8/1/88

FROM:- ROBBIE GOLDSMITH. LES HANOIS LIGHTHOUSE. GUERNSEY. CHANNEL ISLANDS U.K.

TO:- WHO EVER FINDS THIS MESSAGE

THIS MESSAGE WAS THROWN INTO THE SEA FROM THE HANOIS LIGHTHOUSE WHICH IS 2KM OFF THE SOUTH WEST OF GUERNSEY. IF YOU FIND IT, COULD YOU PLEASE WRITE TO SAY WHERE AND WHEN YOU FOUND IT.

THANK YOU (HAPPY NEW YEAR) Robbie.

37. One of the messages sent to sea in bottles by Principal Keeper Robbie Goldsmith. This one didn't go far – it was recovered in Guernsey, not far from Les Hanois lighthouse. (Robbie Goldsmith)

Assistant Keeper Barry Hawkins never arrived at a lighthouse without his home-made wooden box of painting materials. So perhaps it was with an artist's eye that he saw Les Hanois for the first time in 1989. "I remember when I got out there how light and airy it was. The lens was lovely – so small compared with the Smalls, for instance. I was amazed by the amount of rock round the tower where – in the right weather and tide conditions – you could stretch your legs, wander about and get some fresh air."

Barry has exhibited and sold work at Trinity House, London – home of the lighthouse service – the Royal Society of Marine Artists and the King George's Fund for Sailors Exhibitions. And as the specially commissioned

38. This "QSL from Barnacle Bill" was one of the message cards sent out by Principal Keeper Robbie Goldsmith from Les Hanois to other radio enthusiasts. In his spare time Robbie (whose radio "handle" was Barnacle Bill) was an accomplished single side band amateur radio operator; indeed he was once acclaimed world champion for the number of countries contacted. But his activities in the lighthouse ceased when complaints were made about one of his contacts on Guernsey who had inadvertently interfered with aircraft radio traffic. (Robbie Goldsmith)

depiction of Les Hanois reproduced in this book demonstrates, he continues to paint and illustrate.

Ship modelling has also been a favourite hobby of many keepers and mariners and a skilled exponent of this craft was Assistant Keeper Brian Clayton who was photographed in the *Guernsey Evening Press* in December 1978 displaying his fine model of a Swedish warship.

Les Hanois may not rank among the world's most famous lighthouses but one keeper probably did more than anyone else to raise its profile internationally – Principal Keeper Robbie Goldsmith. And he did so in more ways than one.

Goldsmith was a single side band radio enthusiast and during his 14 years in Les Hanois he could often be found contacting other enthusiasts around the world using upper and lower sideband frequencies. Using the handle 'Barnacle Bill', Goldsmith was even acclaimed world champion for the number of countries contacted in a certain period.

In 1988, however, Goldsmith's hobby inadvertently found its way into an official letter of complaint sent to the Department of Trade and Industry's radio investigation service. It appears someone in the northern part of Guernsey using call-sign DB13 was making illegal transmissions – including one to Goldsmith – and causing radio interference for aircraft using the Guernsey airport approach frequency. He recalls that he had received a call saying "Hello Robbie, what's it like out on The Hanois tonight." The monitoring officer did not need to be Sherlock Holmes to track down the recipient of the call, as was confirmed in the letter to the DTI which stated that "we have monitored him in contact with the station at Les Hanois and he is therefore still active and a source of interference to aircraft communications which is a protected service". That radio link was swiftly closed down. Goldsmith also went off the air, following an approach from Trinity House.

But, less controversially, Goldsmith continued to disseminate information and goodwill around the world, but this time by means of the more traditional message in a bottle. Over the years he 'posted' hundreds of these messages, explaining where he was writing from and giving details of the Hanois lighthouse.

In truth many of the bottles were washed up on Guernsey's coast, some in sight of the lighthouse itself. One of the replies now contained in a huge folder of correspondence from around the world says simply: "Dear Robbie, found your bottle on Rocquaine Beach. Didn't get far, did it!! 2kms."

But other bottles were found as far away as Fort Lauderdale in Florida (the message had taken 14 months to get there), the Norwegian fjords and Bremen in Germany. Coincidentally one bottle washed up on a Netherlands beach in January 1986 was found by the owner of the Dutch Lighthouse Museum in the Hook of Holland. Goldsmith was told that the bottle had been picked up in front of the Scheveningen lighthouse! Goldsmith himself has now found a place in a museum for in the lighthouse section of the Guernsey Shipwreck Museum in Fort Grey there is a model of a keeper dressed in one of his old uniforms and sporting a Robbie-type beard. It is an evocative tribute to one of Guernsey's most colourful keepers.

These keepers undoubtedly found solace and satisfaction in these various hobbies and past-times. But for most none of these activities could really compensate for the weeks of separation from wives and families or the lack of creature comforts.

It is true that the routine was occasionally broken by the unexpected delivery of presents or food. For many years pupils of Mare de Carteret School in Guernsey made and delivered special Christmas cakes for the Hanois keepers.

And wives and loved ones were ingenious in transmitting gifts and messages to the lighthouse. Obviously in the latter decades it was easy for families to stay in touch by telephone. However, 'tower to shore' conversations took place before the telephone was installed. The *Guernsey Star* of 29th June 1965 reported on how Mrs Vera Jeffers and Mrs Violet Sythes communicated with their husbands, Principal Keeper Richard Jeffers and Desmond Sythes. In true naval spirit, they used semaphore communication.

Twice a week, between 2pm and 3pm, one or other of the women would walk from the Trinity House Cottages to a pre-arranged point beyond the car park at Pleinmont. Initial contact was made with a flash from a handbag mirror; as the newspaper reported, "the rays from the sun are thus reflected towards the lighthouse and 'dance' across the kitchen wall". This was the signal for the keepers to run down the steps and out on to the landing stage. Then the messages began. White wooden bats were used instead of flags.

The semaphore conversation, which usually continued for about an hour, typically covered mundane domestic topics but occasionally important news was imparted. For instance, this was the way that Mrs Sythes

39. Assistant Keeper Brian Clayton with his fine model of a Swedish warship, photographed in December 1978. (Guernsey Press)

40. Principal Keeper Richard Jeffers (left) and Assistant Keeper L W Humphreys on board the Beacon as they make their way to Les Hanois for their Christmas duty in 1962. Between them can be glimpsed Edwin Martel, one of the boat's crew. (Guernsey Press)

informed her husband that he had been promoted to Principal Keeper and, as a result, would be moving to another station in a month's time.

Visitors were not allowed in the Hanois lighthouse without formal permission although there were undoubtedly a few occasions in fine weather when a wife or loved one was taken by boat for a short visit. Boatman Richard Tostevin recalls one such visit in particular.

"I dropped off the wife and then went off and did some fishing around the tower. To my horror I saw the Trinity House vessel *Patricia* approaching for an unannounced surprise tour of inspection. I shouted a warning to the keepers but there was nothing much that I could do; the inspectors would clearly have seen me picking up a lady in a dress. So I carried on fishing as the Trinity House people arrived for the impromptu inspection. I am sure they were waiting for me to up anchor and go.

"Miraculously they did not spot the wife who had been hidden under a mattress in one of the cots although I am sure they were convinced something was going on." Shortly afterwards – perhaps coincidentally – Trinity House sent out a letter cautioning personnel not to take unauthorised people to the lighthouse.

The Song of the Keeper's Wife

This anonymous poem, published in the Autumn 1968 edition of the Trinity House Service periodical "Flash" could have reflected the feelings of so many wives married to rock station keepers. But I like to think it is especially apposite to the caring wife waiting in her Trinity House cottage at Portelet for her husband serving on the nearby Les Hanois Lighthouse.

Off yonder point there stands a light
Out in the dark and lonely sea,
Where three men watch by day and night,
And one of these my love must be.

For eight long weeks he leaves my side
And all vain thoughts put from his mind
About the life he leads ashore,
About the love he leaves behind.

I walk beside the angry sea,
Watch the tides change from day to day;
The seabirds rise and mock at me,
And I feel my life just slip away.

For when he's home and in my arms
And swears true love for evermore,
I know he'll still return again
And leave me lonely on the shore.

But love is deep and love is strange
It grows more strong each time we part,
I could not wish my man to change,
Although I only share his heart.

This poem was written at a time when keepers served two months on duty with one month off.

CHAPTER NINE

LIFE IN LES HANOIS: ALWAYS THE UNEXPECTED

Principal Keeper Norman Grindle and Assistant Keeper Alan Laing found Guernsey's winter weather especially inhospitable when they arrived on the island for their spell of duty in Les Hanois. Reliefs were usually straightforward – especially once helicopter transfers had been introduced – but this particular one, during the winter of 1989/1990, was going to prove especially memorable. Alan Laing describes the experience:

"When we arrived in Guernsey the night before, the island was to all intents and purposes closed! Snow was quite thick on the ground and continuing to fall and no taxis or buses were operating. I managed to book into the Forest Hotel, next to the airport – I should have been in a hotel in town but there was no way!

"The next morning the snow had stopped falling but the helicopter couldn't get across from England so it was decided to do a boat relief. Norman and I loaded up our gear into the back of the Airport Services van and we had a difficult journey down to the slip at Torteval where we met the boatman, Dick Tostevin. Loading the boat was quite dangerous as we had to carry all our food boxes, stores and personal gear along the full length of the slip. This was tricky underfoot at the best of times but the snow and ice made it more difficult than usual.

"Once loaded we set off for Hanois – conditions weren't too bad, slight swell and very cold but otherwise OK. Halfway there, we were suddenly in a blizzard – the sea picked up and visibility was almost zero in thick, blowing snow. It was probably just as difficult to get back as to carry on so we made for Hanois and were almost upon it before we could see it. The fog signal was sounding but it could hardly be heard until we were almost on top of it.

"We had to sound a hand-held siren to let the keepers know we had arrived – I think they were quite surprised to see us! There was now a very heavy swell and relief was effected by me standing in the bow – one hand on the handrail (it froze to the rail) – and Norman sliding boxes and bags along the deck to me while Dick tried his best to keep the boat as steady as he could.

"As the boat rose on the swell, I would swing a bag or box onto the landing with one hand and 'Peeps' Guest (one of the keepers being relieved) would grab it and pass it back towards the lighthouse. I can't remember how many times we had to do this but it must have taken the best part of an hour.

"Eventually all our gear was on the Hanois and the shore-going gear was on the boat. The transfer of men was twice as tricky but we made it – I'm not sure how I got my hand off the handrail! There was snow on the rocks all around the Hanois – an extremely unusual occurrence. Once we got in we spent a couple of hours just trying to get warm before we tackled any work. A memorable relief!"

This graphic description illustrates the risks taken down the decades as successive boatmen battled to make transfer of men and goods in seas and currents that at best were uncertain and at worst terrifying.

Robbie Goldsmith remembers the day that boatman Tostevin saved his life in another hazardous transfer operation. Again in was a winter's day. "Cyril Jackson, a maintenance guy, and Dave Wilson, an electrician, wanted to get ashore. It was getting close to Christmas.

"It was awful weather – it must have been blowing six or seven. Dick came out in the *Pamela* and we managed to get Cyril and Dave on board. I was passing some equipment to them when I must have slipped. I went straight in and straight down. It was freezing. I can't swim so I grabbed hold of the fender at the front of the boat." There was a danger that Goldsmith would be crushed between the bucking boat and the landing stage so Tostevin reversed the vessel away from the rocks.

"I don't know how he did it, but Dick rushed forward and grabbed me by the seat of my pants and hauled me out. I must have weighed a ton... I suppose the adrenalin worked for Dick."

Richard Tostevin has his own memories: "You get huge seas out there. At times you couldn't see the top of the lighthouse; the swells were so big. I remember one occasion – probably the roughest trip I made – when we had to deliver a small parcel with metal flanges. We had to enter white water to get near the tower. With John de La Mare, the 'postman', we managed to throw a rope to the keepers who were standing on top of the landing, by the door. They then hauled in the parcel.

"Delivering supplies in heavy seas was no fun. I remember one day when it was really rough and we had to take out water in five gallon drums. I couldn't figure out how we were going to land these heavy drums... it was blowing a gale. Fortunately my wife Pamela, who was with me, had a brainwave. We tied the drums to a line, played them out and then floated them on to the rocks."

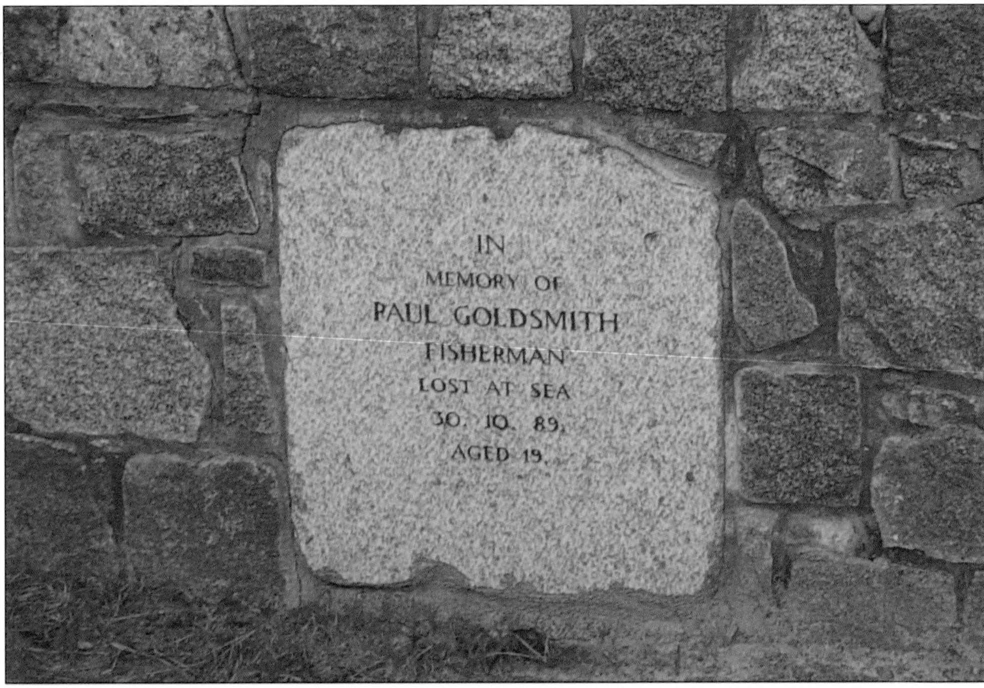

41. The waterside memorial to the memory of Paul Goldsmith, the 19-year-old son of Hanois keeper Robbie Goldsmith, who was drowned while fishing close to the lighthouse. The memorial, set into the harbour wall at Torteval, was made from recovered granite that had originally been destined for use in the construction of Les Hanois lighthouse. (Author)

Bad weather and temperamental seas could always be relied on to interfere with the routine and monotony of life in Les Hanois. In May 1865 an inspection committee from Trinity House reported in a matter-of-fact way that it had been "delayed a little" by a heavy squall, with lightning and rain. Another Trinity House report, of October 10th 1871 refers to "recent gales" causing damage to the "cement walk" at Les Hanois.

In the following 130 years or so there would be repeated incidences of such damage caused to the landing and steps. In March 1967 no less than 10 granite steps were washed away by waves. One of the keepers reported that the waves had been 40 feet high and spray had gone over the top of the tower. And in April 1990 it was reported that a section of the east landing along with part of the helipad decking had been washed away in severe winter storms.

In March 1901 a plumber from St Martin's in Guernsey – a Mr Le Mesurier – was reported to have been detained on the Hanois for nine days due to bad weather. At times the waves were said to have reached the height of the lantern, as they have done on a number of occasions since.

When he finally returned to shore Mr Le Mesurier, who had been fitting the "latest sanitary improvements", reported that during the storms the lighthouse had been struck by lightning, causing a pane of glass three-eighths of an inch thick, to be cracked with "a report like a gun".

Principal Keeper Tommy Cuthbertson and Assistant Keeper H Curnow were less fortunate in January 1952. Having completed their two month tour of duty they found themselves trapped in the lighthouse for a further three weeks by storms and rough seas. The *Guernsey Star* reported that the previous record for an overdue relief had been 18 days.

Waiting to relieve the two were Assistant Keepers Tom Whiston and Simon Reynolds. Tom and his wife had celebrated Christmas early – on December 16 – in their Trinity House cottage in anticipation of the relief two days later. But as the storms set in they were able to celebrate again on Christmas Day itself. Mrs Whiston was fully accustomed to the uncertain life of a lighthouse keeper – her father and both her grandfathers had been keepers and she herself had been born at Start Point lighthouse in Devon.

It is testament to the design and builders of Les Hanois lighthouse that the tower itself has never been damaged by the fierce storms or huge seas that have repeatedly battered that south west corner of Guernsey.

While feeling safe inside the tower the keepers could not escape the noise and sheer menace of the storm raging outside. Robbie Goldsmith again provides some insight, describing conditions on the night of January 21st 1984 when the freighter *Radient Med* was wrecked off Guernsey's St Martin's Point. "I was with Bert Tromans and Mark Shipley. We were listening to the May Day radio call. It was a ferocious night. Suddenly a window in the lower engine room was smashed open. Solid green water burst through, cascading down stairs and washing stores down with it.

That window – with a frame made of gun metal – was over 45 feet high!"

Paul Davis will never forget the night of the big storm in October 1987, the "hurricane" that caused so much damage throughout much of southern Britain. "The noise was horrendous. I was sitting next to Robbie on the curved bench and it was really difficult to hear each other. It sounded like a steam train." But Davis never felt insecure or threatened in Les Hanois. "It was solid as a rock." This seems in marked contrast to one of his other postings, Wolf Rock. "That used to shake in violent storms; I remember I sometimes slept with my lifebelt on in my early days in Wolf Rock."

Safe as it might have been, Les Hanois may not have been everyone's choice of a haven in a storm, as was proved in the 1980s when three direct labour force employees were sent by Trinity House in Penzance to do some work in the tower. It was blowing a gale when one of the men complained of pains. When the symptoms were relayed by telephone to a doctor it was thought he may have appendicitis. Given the severe weather two Sea King helicopters were flown from Culdrose in Cornwall to assist in the medical evacuation.

On arrival at Les Hanois, a Royal Navy doctor was winched down to the tower where he examined the complaining workman. It was found there was nothing physically wrong with the man; he just wanted to leave. To make matters worse the workman had the cheek to ask the doctor for a lift back to Cornwall, where he lived. The doctor was not amused, to say the least. The incident had left the whole of Devon and Cornwall without air-sea rescue cover.

Inevitably, there have been times when it has been necessary to evacuate keepers from Hanois on medical grounds. It happened to Robbie Goldsmith twice, once on account of raging toothache. Paul Davis recalls that he had been asked to use a pair of pliers to extract the offending tooth but it was agreed that a dentist would do a more professional job. Goldsmith was taken ashore by boat and had the treatment; it was just as well as the treatment was needed for a different tooth than the one his colleague had been asked to extract. The return journey was another of those eventful transfers. The normal lighthouse boatmen were not available so some fishermen returned Goldsmith to the Hanois. Perhaps because they were unaccustomed to the currents around the tower the fishermen found their boat being swept up on to the landing stage, endangering all inside the vessel. Fortunately, the boat was refloated on a following wave.

The other medical evacuation hit the headlines – "Lightkeeper airlift after acid splash" was the *Guernsey Evening Post* description of the incident in June 1987. Goldsmith had been checking the batteries at about midnight. "I was using the hydrometer but unfortunately when I squeezed it I found that the rubber had perished and some of the alkaline solution went into my eyes. We had satchets of water for such an emergency and I quickly washed my eyes."

After the local doctor had been contacted, Trinity House and Brixham coastguard arranged for a helicopter airlift by the French rescue service Crossma. Goldsmith was rushed to Princess Elizabeth Hospital in Guernsey. "But for the prompt action I think I could have gone blind." There was a happy, if unexpected sequel to this drama: "The incident attracted quite a lot of publicity. It wasn't too long before I started getting a lot of letters, especially from women!"

42. Fisherman Paul Goldsmith on his way to visit Les Hanois lighthouse. Paul, the son of Principal Keeper Robbie Goldsmith, tragically died at sea, close to the lighthouse, in October 1989. He was 19 years old. (Robbie Goldsmith)

A terrible and particularly poignant tragedy occurred on Monday, October 30th, 1989 when Robbie Goldsmith's 19-year-old son Paul died at sea, perhaps in sight of Les Hanois lighthouse. It was a loss felt by everyone connected with the lighthouse.

Paul Goldsmith lived for the sea. He used to "bunk" off school in order to go fishing. And when, as a teenager, he acquired his own boat, he was a frequent visitor to the Hanois keepers, delivering mail, crabs and the like. "He was a friend of so many keepers," said his father. "I have so many happy memories of Paul."

43. Principal Keeper Richard Jeffers waves to friends ashore as he goes out to Les Hanois for another spell of duty in 1962. (Guernsey Press)

Exactly how Paul lost his life is not known. The sea was lumpy; a swell was running. Old fishermen say the “sea is working” on such a day. A fisherman, married with a young wife, he had motored out into Rocquaine Bay in his small boat to bring in his crab pots for the winter. He recovered the pots but what happened afterwards will always remain a mystery. The boat was later found with the engine still in gear and it is assumed that a rogue sea spilled the young fisherman into the cold sea.

A search was started at 7pm that evening – six hours after he had departed on this short fishing trip – but he was nowhere to be seen. It was not until December 17th that his body was found at nearby L’Éree.

There is a waterside memorial to the memory of Paul, set into the harbour wall at Torteval. Appropriately it is made from recovered granite that had originally been destined for use in the construction of Les Hanois lighthouse.

44. This cartoon by Hanois boatman Richard Tostevin recalls one of the instances when the lighthouse plumbing went awry. As he remembers it two men spent five weeks trying to sort out the problem. Eventually a hole was dug at the bottom of the tower. “Both men were in this hole when they managed to clear the blockage. You can imagine the state they were in... 80 feet of pressure bearing down. They were well covered. It was not pleasant.” (R Tostevin)

45. High wire act for a steeplejack fitting a lightning conductor to Les Hanois lighthouse in 1985 (R Tostevin)

CHAPTER TEN
LIGHTHOUSE UNDER OCCUPATION

The German occupation of the Channel Islands during the Second World War had both surprising and inevitable consequences for Les Hanois lighthouse.

In the early days of the war there was clearly bewilderment on the part of islanders that while they were dutifully adhering to 'black out' rules, the Hanois light was still shining. As the *Guernsey Evening Press* of September 5th 1939 reported: "Many residents on the west coast last night stressed the fact that during periods of 'black out' the Hanois lighthouse is displaying full beam." In response, Captain J Penstone Franklin, the Guernsey Harbourmaster, responded that the local authorities had no power over lighthouses as they were entirely under the control of Trinity House.

The questions continued to be aired in the newspapers and repeatedly it was explained that the lights came under international maritime law. But the residents – at that time still free from occupation – were assured an "effective decision" would be taken in the near future.

In fact the Hanois light was not extinguished until June the following year. This followed a decision by the British government, on June 19th, to demilitarise Guernsey. The British authorities had concluded that the Channel Islands held little strategic value; essentially Guernsey was being left to its fate. By the end of the month, the island was occupied. This was a particularly traumatic time for all islanders.

The lighthouse keepers' exit from Hanois, on the afternoon of the 21st was inevitably hasty. Unused oil and fog signal explosives – some of them kept at Fort Grey – were just abandoned. The men were picked up by the Trinity House vessel *Vestal* that had been engaged in removing all the Channel Island keepers from their stations.

47. Les Hanois lighthouse surrounded by breaking waves in the winter of 1984. (Guernsey Press)

approached Alderney's Casquets lighthouse in dinghies during the dead of night. Seven Germans on duty in the lighthouse were captured and whisked away in the dinghies, but not before radios and spare equipment had been destroyed and code books and diaries had been taken.

The Führer not only asked for details of the attack, but he also ordered a study of lighthouse defences in general. This led to recommendations that these lighthouses should be protected with mines and barbed wire, permanent ladders should be removed and special alarm systems should be installed. Les Hanois became even more of a fortress.

Guernseyman Gerald Edwards captured the feelings of islanders during this period in his wonderfully evocative novel "The Book of Ebenezer Le Page". The fictitious trio of Raymond, Horace and Lisa are at Pleinmont, at the western end of the island. "'Let's go as far as the two big rocks,' he (Horace) said to Raymond. 'I want to see the Hanois light.' 'It isn't lit!' she screamed at them. 'Isn't that just like two fools of men: to go and look for a light that isn't there!' Horace flung the door open, and stood with his fist up, the big fool. 'It will be lit again!' he said. 'Guernsey is our island, not theirs; and we will go where we like on it!'"

True enough, the Les Hanois light was lit again... but not until the night of September 18th 1945, several months after the end of the war and after the Channel Islands had been liberated.

The lighthouse itself even had a bit part to play in that liberation. On May 7th the BBC announced that Victory in Europe Day (VE Day) would be celebrated the following day but Vice-Admiral Friedrich Hüffmeier, Germany's Commander-in-Chief of the Islands, appeared to be unmoved. Hüffmeier was still seeking terms for an armistice and there were fears that he might decide to fight on alone.

A signal was sent to him saying that he must be aware of the German surrender. It proposed that his representative should rendezvous four miles south of Les Hanois light to sign an instrument of surrender. Hüffmeier replied that his accredited representative would be at the Hanois at noon on May 8th.

Brigadier Alfred Snow, head of 'Operation Nestegg' to liberate the Channel Islands, left Plymouth with other officers in HMS *Bulldog* and HMS *Beagle* and sailed for Guernsey to affect the handover. They duly rendezvoused with a German mine-sweeping trawler at the appointed hour only to find that Hüffmeier was continuing to be intransigent. He had sent a junior naval officer who was mandated to do no more than discuss armistice terms. What is more the German officer – under instruction from Hüffmeier – warned the British contingent that as the general cease-fire was not due to take effect until 00.01 the following day they should withdraw or risk being fired upon.

As midnight approached there was another rendezvous off the Hanois but this time Brig. Snow, knowing that the cease fire was about to take effect, elected to move to St Peter Port. The surrender was duly signed on the quarterdeck of HMS *Bulldog* at 7.14 on the morning of the 9th.

Eight days later Trinity House officers visited Les Hanois, as well as the other island lighthouses in the area. Although it was found that the large optic had been damaged by gunfire, the lights and machinery were deemed to be in reasonably good working order and it was decided they should all be reinstated as quickly as possible.

In the event it was another four months before the Hanois light shone again. The Trinity House Lighthouse Service station book for Hanois records that the light and fog signals were brought into operation on the night of September 18th/19th 1945. It was also noted that the keepers were to receive special allowance of two shillings per day each for additional cleaning and painting work needed to restore the lighthouse to a "reasonable condition".

Under the headline "The Beacons Gleam", the *Guernsey Weekly Press* and *Advertiser* reported that Trinity House vessels – the *Patricia* and the *André Blondel* – had been kept busy in the "reconditioning and revictualling" operation needed to get the Hanois lighthouse functioning. The newspaper pointed out that this operation had become of "great importance" given that shipping had to be diverted around the west and south coasts of Guernsey owing to the presence of mines in the normal shipping channels to the north.

As always, the weather had an influence on the proceedings. Retired Hanois keeper, R J Simon, recalled in the Trinity House periodical *Flash* in 1989 that at the end of the war he was one of a party of three who were taken to the lighthouse in the *Patricia*. The trio were there to assist the new Principal Keeper Cyril Trezise and two new Assistant Keepers – recruited locally – and to "instruct them in the ways of the station". Simon recalled that they were to remain in the lighthouse for two days but had to stay for nine on account of bad weather.

It was to be a few years before the Trinity House cottages at Pleinmont were fully restored. Like many other buildings on the island, these keepers' quarters were gutted during the occupation and the early post war keepers and their families were forced to live elsewhere. Fortunately the shell of the homes remained intact. The cottages still stand today, proud and handsome, although no longer occupied by Trinity House personnel.

The Hanois light may have been restored to its pre-war glory but the legacy of occupation remained. German names – such as 'A S Kreber', 'A Ziggler', and 'K Weber' – incised into the Hanois rocks below the lighthouse bore testament to those who had served – or maybe had been held captive – in the rock tower during the war. There are many stories, perhaps some apocryphal, of the lighthouse being used as a punishment cell, even as solitary confinement, by the German military. A persistent story relates to indentations in the ceiling of the service room. These marks are said to have been made by a bullet fired by a suicidal prisoner although how he came by the weapon is not known.

Apocryphal or not the "suicide" seems to have had an effect on Principal Keeper Norman Wakley. He says that while he had heard about the shooting he neither looked for nor saw the tell-tale bullet mark. "What I do know is that I always felt very queer when I slept in the bunk I originally had, between the door and the window. I am not saying it had anything to do with the Germans being there but I had a definite feeling of unease. When one of the keepers left and I shifted into his bunk I know I felt much better there."

48. Trinity House Cottages at Pleinmont as they look now. Like many other buildings on the island, the cottages were gutted during the German occupation in the 1939-45 war. It took several years after the liberation for the dwellings to be fully restored. (Author)

CHAPTER ELEVEN
END OF AN ERA

Thursday, January 4th 1996, was like so many winter days in Guernsey – mild, damp and windy; so windy that the Island Commodore ferry had problems in docking. The sea was rough. Showery rainfall on the island had reached just 0.13 inches and the maximum temperature was 50°F (10°C) making it one of the mildest spots in the UK.

There was little news of note on the island. Motor traders rejected calls for Sunday opening and a "missing" Sark man was found safe and well. Elsewhere in the UK the chief executive of the London Stock Exchange was dismissed, police expressed their fear about a stalker troubling the Princess Royal, and Tony Blair – as leader of the Opposition – was promising that a future Labour Government would attract foreign investment through low tax and low inflation.

But for Britain's rock towers controlled by Trinity House the day also marked the end of an era; the day that lighthouses became fully automatic.

Les Hanois was the last rock tower lighthouse to be "demanned", an ugly, dehumanising word that describes the march of progress whereby computers and mechanical equipment are deemed to be more cost effective than humans. For the lighthouse keepers lifted by helicopter from Les Hanois for the very last time it was a bitter sweet occasion.

There was a modicum of pomp. The last watch – Principal Keeper Dave Appleby and Assistant Keepers Dave McGovern and Peter Boulton – had been joined in the tower by Captain Peter King, one of Trinity House's Elder Brethren. There was a simple log signing ceremony and last minute housekeeping chores to complete before the quartet prepared to climb the vertical fixed ladder to the lantern roof and then the helideck for the short helicopter ride to Guernsey Airport. First to leave were Captain King and Peter Boulton. They were followed later in the morning by Dave McGovern and Dave Appleby.

Their departure was something of an anticlimax for over the previous day or two the keepers had attracted a good deal of media attention. Press, radio and TV crews all wanted interviews with the last of the rock tower lighthouse keepers.

Leyla Linton wrote in *The Times* that the three keepers looked "tired and pleased to be leaving" as they were taken off the lighthouse by helicopter. Her report said that Dave Appleby, who had entered the profession 29 years previously when oil lamps were still providing the light, had mixed feelings about leaving Les Hanois. "It was my home for six months of the year," he was quoted as saying. "I felt glad to be going, but also sad. It was a very special experience and a way of life, a Victorian way of life.

"Lighthouse keepers who work offshore get a lot of respect from those who work onshore because it was just much tougher. Recently we have been surrounded by rough seas and fog, which is quite unusual. It made us feel more isolated."

Dave McGovern remembers he felt very much the same: "It was a sad day, knowing that from then on keepers would not be going to sea again." Coincidentally, he had been one of the last keepers to leave the Royal Sovereign in 1994.

"Sadness" was a much used word at that time. "It's a little bit sad, but then again that's progress," Dave Appleby told the *Guernsey Evening Press* in another of his interviews. "It is sort of inevitable. Because of all the technology there is now, they have to use it. But every lighthouse that gets automated is another nail in the coffin." He pointed out that the keepers were not only losing their livelihoods but also their homes in the Trinity House cottages. Indeed, it would not be long before Trinity House sold these homes into the local Guernsey housing market.

Six keepers knew they were facing redundancy although Dave Appleby first went to St Catherine's in the Isle of Wight, Peter Boulton was transferred to Portland Bill in Dorset and Dave McGovern was moved to nearby Alderney.

As *The Times* pointed out, new technology and a desire to save money had seen the start of the conversion programme for automation back in 1982. It was costing over £100,000 a year to keep Les Hanois fully manned.

The £315,000 automation of lighthouses had been made possible by developments in telemetry and computerisation. But there was a further

49. A helicopter departs from Les Hanois lighthouse with a sling of goods in January 1996, shortly before the last keepers leave and the tower is automated. (Guernsey Press)

advance which placed Les Hanois on an even more independent footing. Later that year, in 1996 – just 32 years after diesel-generated electricity had been installed in the tower – Les Hanois became the first rock tower to be fitted with photovoltaic panels. The installation work was undertaken by Trinity House's engineering department in Cowes, Isle of Wight.

There are 38 solar panels circling the tower. These solar arrays comprise AEG MQ36D solar photovoltaic modules mounted vertically in two rows on the outside of the helideck support structure. Together they have a maximum output of 2,014 watts – comfortably sufficient to charge the two sets of 12 batteries. The 24 volt batteries themselves power the main light, fog signal and the lighthouse facilities system; for example telemetry, the internal lighting and the control system. The battery systems are designed to have a reserve capacity of 15 days for the main light, fog and facilities system and five days for the emergency system.

At the same time as the solar panels were installed changes were made in the light's character to keep the power requirement low enough for the new solarisation and to increase the length of the flash to achieve the required 20-mile range. So a new two position lampchanger with 35 watt metal arc lamps was installed within the existing optic, the rotation of which was slowed down. The character of the light was changed from two white flashes every five seconds to two every 13 seconds.

The existing air fog signal was also replaced by a single directional electric emitter stack installed in a west facing space left in the ring of solar panels. The fog signal is controlled by an automatic fog detector.

All these operations are now monitored and controlled through the Trinity House Operations Control Centre on The Quay at Harwich by means of a telemetry link through cellular radio. Today monitoring officers keep a constant vigil at the computer screens checking the integrity of Les Hanois and the other 71 lighthouses for which it is responsible in England, Wales and the Channel Islands. There are both visual and audible alerts to signify any problems; essential items of equipment, such as the light and optic drive, are duplicated to ensure there is no interruption to the warning signals. Maintenance work is carried out by Trinity House's Penzance depot.

At the time of the Les Hanois automation in 1996 Trinity House said the implementation of central control and monitoring would enable savings of £1,374,000 to be achieved over the following 15 years.

But financial savings come at a human cost, as the keepers had pointed out. And they were not alone. The Hanois boatman, Richard Tostevin is still required to carry people and supplies to and from the lighthouse on the odd occasion but it is nothing like at the frequency he enjoyed in his early days of service. He became the official boatman in 1974 since when he has served the lighthouse in five different vessels – *Paula Joanne, Royella, Pamela* (named after his wife), *Portelet* (which under a different name and owner was once used for covert Secret Service operations), and the present boat *Abalone.*

Richard Tostevin told reporters covering the "demanning" of the lighthouse that day in January 1996: "We are always sorry to see people leave. It's not something that we have been looking forward to. I think it's going to be even sadder to see the Hanois empty. There will be attendants going there from time to time but it will never be quite the same."

Sharing his feelings was the Trinity House representative on Guernsey, John de la Mare. Then aged 57 and known as the 'Hanois Postman' John de La Mare had started making trips to Hanois when he was 14. "I used to be known as Johnny the Postman, taking over parcels and fresh cakes baked by the keepers' wives. They used to spend two months at a time on there, sometimes three if the weather was bad," he recalled.

"Its going to be a sad day for safety because there's no one out there if you're fishing and something goes wrong," he added. He was echoing the feelings of a number of islanders and maritime visitors.

Trinity House insisted, however, that with automation safety would be the same or even better, a point made today. When I visited Harwich, Duty Officer Gordon Head pointed out that all essential equipment was monitored every minute of every day. Maintenance was rigorous. "Everything we do in this centre is concerned with the interest of the mariner," said Head, an ex mariner himself.

Back in 1996 *Yachting Monthly* was not convinced. It reported on the concern and sadness engendered by automation, and stated that Trinity House had pointed out "the keepers' job was to look after the light and not out at the surrounding area".

Strictly speaking this is true. However, there are a number of occasions when the sharp eyes of Hanois keepers had come to the aid of fishermen and sailors in trouble.

Indeed, Trinity House's own periodical *"Flash"* reported that on the evening of July 9th, 1988, Assistant Keeper Mike Williams had spotted a

50. The Trinity House vessel Patricia on her last voyage of inspection to Guernsey, photographed at St Peter Port in 1980. (Guernsey Press)

51. End of an era. Keepers Dave McGovern (left) and Dave Appleby leave the helicopter after departing from Les Hanois for the very last time. The original newspaper caption to this photograph was headed "Between a rock and the next place". (Guernsey Press)

distress flare put up from the cabin cruiser *Monoleen,* sinking one mile WSW of the lighthouse. Mike Williams immediately replied with a four star white rocket and then informed St Peter Port radio. Guernsey lifeboat was mobilised, arriving at the stricken cruiser just 45 minutes after the alarm had been raised.

Principal Keeper Norman Wakley recalls another incident involving a yacht in trouble, although this time there was far less drama. "One evening one of the keepers – I think it was Ralph Humphries – saw a yacht going on to the rocks. The people got off the yacht into a rubber dinghy. The yacht then went between the rocks. When it was clear they caught up with it and got back on board and sailed off!"

There was much more drama at Christmas in 1973 when the 856 feet long bulk carrier *Elwood Mead* was driven on to Les Grunes de Nord-Ouest rocks, north west of Guernsey while on her maiden voyage from Western Australia. Robbie Goldsmith, who was Assistant Keeper at the time,

52. This cartoon by Hanois boatman Richard Tostevin sums up his feelings about the lighthouse automation in January 1996. He told reporters covering the "demanning" of the lighthouse: "We are always sorry to see people leave. It's not something that we have been looking forward to. I think it's going to be even sadder to see the Hanois empty. There will be attendants going there from time to time but it will never be quite the same." (R Tostevin)

remembers waking up and looking out of the window and seeing "all these lights". "I couldn't tell whether it was an oil tanker or ore carrier, but it was big. I called up St Peter Port radio and reported there was a ship aground with all its lights on. The operator replied: 'Happy Christmas Robbie... have you been drinking?'" Fortunately, there were no casualties, in sharp contrast to the cargo vessel *Prosperity* which was lost with all hands – 18 crew – very close by a few days later. Norman Wakley was another who remembers that Christmas: "*The Elwood Mead* was quite a sight; we watched as they tried to tow her off."

It was the wreck of Liberian cargo vessel *La Salle* in 1965 that led to an unusual and dramatic rescue involving Les Hanois boatman, Richard Tostevin. It is a story of real heroism and one previously untold. The drama is here recounted in Richard Tostevin's own words:

"There was one occasion in the 1960s when I agreed to visit the central portion – the bridge – of the submerged wreck of *La Salle* off the west coast of Guernsey with these two guys who were sailing around the world on a big yacht, *Starship Two,* berthed in St Peter Port. I was in my 28 foot long fishing boat *L'Agile* which had a French engine with a temperamental gear shift. It often slipped out of neutral.

"I boarded the bridge of the wreck with one of the guys – Larry – leaving his mate standing by in my boat. We had just found a lamp on *La Salle* when, to my horror I saw the guy had slipped off my boat and fallen in the water. The engine had gone into reverse and the boat was disappearing fast under power and the influence of the tide. The guy was treading water but in a terrible state. Then Larry told me he was recovering from polio.

"We both tried to swim to him but it was cold and the Devil had got me by the ankle. I couldn't make any headway. I shouted to Larry that we ought to get back to the *La Salle*. By now the distressed guy was a couple of hundred yards away and our boat was disappearing fast. Larry and I started ripping off anything that would float – doors and timber – from *La Salle* and floated these down with the tide to the guy. This worked but he was still in a bad way. He was calling out 'Help! Come and get me!' I remember we stripped the aerial from *La Salle* and using a door for a float I started paddling towards the guy as Larry played out the aerial wire. Fortunately the wire was long enough. I got to the chap and to quieten him down I hit him. It was no gentle pat, but I had no choice. Gradually we made it back to the wreck although I had been very worried that the wire would snag.

"But then what were we going to do? We had no way of getting ashore... my boat was long gone. We looked around for something to make a fire and luckily found a big magnifying glass. As it was sunny we managed to light a fire and we burned as much rubber as we could find to make smoke.

"As it happens we saw a boat coming towards us. It was George Le Couteur, the then Hanois boatman – my predecessor – taking out a group of sightseers. He managed to get us aboard and agreed to go out and chase down L'Agile which was by now miles away, given the influence of the tides. Eventually we got back on board *L'Agile* and before dropping the guys back to St Peter Port I managed to do a bit of diving off the south coast. I remember I caught 14 crayfish.

"It was, as they say, all in a day's work."

53. Monitoring officer Karen Potter keeps vigil at the computer screens, checking the integrity of Les Hanois and other lighthouses in England, Wales and the Channel Islands at the Trinity House Operations Control Centre on The Quay at Harwich. (Author)

CHAPTER TWELVE

WRECKED AROUND THE HANOIS

Historic shipwrecks off Guernsey's west coast prompted the initial calls for a lighthouse at Les Hanois. Further shipwrecks in the 19th century reinforced the pro-lighthouse campaign when there was a concerted movement in opposition. And, paradoxically, even after the lighthouse had been built, shipwrecks continued to occur, reinforcing the dangers of that part of Guernsey's coast. Who is to say how many more vessels would have been wrecked but for the presence of Les Hanois lighthouse?

Henry Tupper, who was one of the leading lighthouse protagonists, compiled a list of 16 major wrecks that had occurred in that vicinity in the period December 30th 1835 to December 19th 1849. He presented this list to the French Consul General in London, recognising that French shipping in particular were imperilled by sea and weather conditions off Guernsey's west coast. As we have seen Henry Tupper was to become the highly influential chairman of Guernsey's lighthouse committee.

Historian J M David, in his paper 'The Early History of the Hanois Lighthouse', published in 1960 recorded 20 total losses in the area between Les Hanois and Richmond, in Perelle Bay, on Guernsey's south west coast in the years 1816 to 1862, when the first light was exhibited. He counted a further nine total losses between 1862 and 1932. It was noted that besides the total losses there were many cases of ships striking and eventually getting off again.

The results of my own researches in roughly the same area, although extended slightly to include an adjacent part of the south coast, are summarised in the following appendix. These indicate there were 64 wrecks on or close to Hanois Rocks in the period prior to December 1862 and 53 since the light first shone there. It has to be conceded, of course, that this list can never be complete or, for that matter, wholly accurate.

While maritime research is constantly revealing new information it must be accepted that we will never know the true extent of the tragedies and accidents that have occurred down the centuries.

Some of the wrecks that were used in evidence by those campaigning for a lighthouse have already been described; for instance, *HMS Boreas* in 1807, the Danis dogre *Marie Elizabeth* in 1816, the brig *Five Sisters* in 1848, the packet ship *Oneida* in 1849, the schooner-galliot *Constant* in 1860, and the schooner-brig *Globe* shortly before the lighthouse became operational in 1862.

One tragic wreck that has been fixed in the memories of Les Hanois duty keepers and those in the rescue services occurred in terrifying conditions on the night of January 16th 1974. A Cypriot cargo ship, *mv Prosperity* battered by hurricane-strength winds and huge seas, was driven on to La Conchée reef, a jagged outcrop some three miles north east of Les Hanois lighthouse. Everyone on board – 17 men and a young woman – died, drowned in what must have been a maelstrom. It is the worst sea tragedy in Guernsey since the 1939-45 war.

The small 2,088 tons freighter was on passage from Finland to Greece when she encountered engine failure in the midst of a violent storm. Throughout the day ships had been taking shelter around the British and French coasts but now the *Prosperity* found herself helpless at the mercy of the elements. Her Greek captain, Georgios Kastellorizios sent a distress call to the signal station at St Peter Port, reporting that the ship was 20 miles west of Les Hanois and turning and spinning helplessly. He appealed for a tug and lifeboat, adding, it is reported: "If you hear nothing further from us you will know we have abandoned ship."

Several ships and the St Peter Port lifeboat, *Sir William Arnold,* responded to the call but they were unable to locate *Prosperity* in the vicinity of her reported position. The lifeboat was recalled, given that the conditions were so bad and visibility so poor.

Police patrolled the coastline during the night and at first light the *Properity* was spotted on the reef, broken in two and with no sign of life. "It had been a terrible, terrible night," recalled Norman Wakley, who as Principal Keeper, had been on duty at Les Hanois throughout the drama. "We watched as the ship broke up and we couldn't do anything. It was terrible."

Sixteen bodies were recovered from the sea although the Master and the boatswain, Uzoglan Ibrahim, were never found. Among those who died

54. The wrecked Cypriot cargo ship Prosperity that was lost with all hands after being driven on to La Conchée reef, on Guernsey's west coast, in hurricane-force winds on the night of January 16th 1974. . "It had been a terrible, terrible night," recalled Norman Wakley, who as Principal Keeper, had been on duty at Les Hanois throughout the drama. "We watched as the ship broke up and we couldn't do anything. It was terrible." (Guernsey Press)

was 21-year-old Gloria Pagratis, the assistant steward and the only woman on board. She was the wife of the second engineer Sfyridon Pagratis who also lost his life. A photograph, presumed to show their marriage ceremony, was among the crew's possessions washed ashore. At one point there was concern that there might have been a baby on board the *Prosperity,* concern that was heightened when baby clothing and a doll were found on Cobo beach, but this was later discounted.

The majority of the recovered bodies were buried in Guernsey, some being given the appropriate Islamic or Sikh rights. The Mission to Seamen Society raised funds to erect a permanent memorial to the loss of Prosperity and her crew; it stands at L'Éree, a headland between La Conchée reef and Les Hanois.

A huge quantity of timber from the *Prosperity* was washed ashore on that fateful day. Hundreds of islanders collected what they could, prompting a warning in the *Guernsey Evening Press* that "in view of the recent frequent shipwrecks around these islands, readers are reminded that they are not legally entitled to goods washed ashore or taken from vessels driven ashore". The timber that was recovered legally was later sold in a public offering.

A few days after the shipwreck, His Excellency Costas Ashiotis, London-based High Commissioner for Cyprus, expressed his country's thanks and appreciation to the people and life-saving services of Guernsey for the aid and assistance that had been rendered.

Hanois boatman, Richard Tostevin, has provided a footnote to the *Prosperity* tragedy. He believes the lives of the crew might have been saved if they had remained with the vessel, rather than abandoning ship. As he said: "The charts were later recovered – and they were dry." He adds that there was a further fatality arising from the *Prosperity* wreck. "A Jersey man died when his speed boat hit drift wood from the ship."

That winter demonstrated that in spite of well positioned lighthouses and the most up-to-date navigational aids, shipwrecks will always occur. For only a few days before the *Prosperity* was driven ashore, the bulk carrier *Elwood Mead* had run hard aground on the nearby Les Grunes de Nord-Ouest. The ship, over 856 feet long was on her maiden voyage from Port Dampier in Western Australia with 122,954 tons of iron ore when, on Christmas Day, she was another victim of that winter's storms. Fortunately there was no loss of life – only extensive damage.

This was the ship that keeper Robbie Goldsmith had reported being aground with "all its lights on", only to be teased for having too much Christmas tipple. In his website memories, Principal Keeper Harold Taylor recalls an unexpected visit to the stranded ship. Bristow helicopters had been contracted to ferry pumps to the bulk carrier. "Early that morning we were due ashore, and it was hoped that she would float clear, but it was not to be, which in some ways led to a new experience for us because our relief chopper was prevented from leaving Cornwall. The temporarily locally based chopper was requested to take us ashore. In doing so it had to call at the Elwood and we landed on her deck. The next high water they were in fact able to float clear."

55. The partially-completed ship, Vermontborg, attracted many sightseers as she lay stranded high and dry on La Capelle Reef – not far from Les Hanois lighthouse – in January 2003. The engine-less vessel was being towed from the Black Sea to Holland when her towlines parted in rough weather. After resting on the rocks for 16 days she was finally towed free on a very high tide and taken to Harlingen in the Netherlands where she was fitted out. (Author)

It had taken two months after the original grounding, to make seaworthy and refloat the *Elwood Mead*. She was then towed to Rotterdam. There the ship that had originally cost £13 million was declared a constructive total loss and sold for £8.25 million to Greek shipping interests. Following extensive refitting she was renamed *Good Leader.*

Another notable post war wreck was that of *La Salle,* a Liberian vessel, off the west coast of Guernsey. The wreck was the site of boatman Richard Tostevin's heroism, recounted earlier. The 4,560 tons ship had struck Sambule and Soufleuresse rocks in rough seas during a May night in 1965 as she was carrying a cargo of oats from South Australia to Hamburg.

56. The wreck of the Liberian cargo vessel La Salle that came to grief off the west coast of Guernsey in 1965. It was this wreck that was the site of an unusual and dramatic rescue involving Les Hanois boatman Richard Tostevin. (Guernsey Press)

The Master, Douglas Trail, called for assistance, reporting that there was a hole in the engine room. The rescued crew later spoke of a "great shudder" as the vessel struck the reef. Conditions were difficult – rough seas, a stiff breeze and poor visibility – but all of the crew of 39, as well Captain Trail's wife, Molly, were rescued by St Peter Port lifeboat, under Coxswain Captain John Petit.

Perhaps the most harrowing account of an historic Hanois wreck concerns an American ship, the *Bostonian.* It is a story containing all the elements of a dramatic shipwreck – severe weather, the selfless rescue of another vessel in distress, a valuable vessel pounded to destruction on perilous rocks, personal heroism and tragic loss of life. And it all happened in January 1861 in sight of the emerging Les Hanois lighthouse, then under construction. As *The Star* newspaper reported, had the lighthouse been finished, the accident would not have occurred.

The *Bostonian* was on a passage from New York to London with a cargo of flour, cheese and other goods. Her Master, Charles Brookman, was unsure of the vessel's exact position because bad weather had allowed only three navigational sightings. It had been a "boisterous" passage; severe gales had followed in succession and on December 24th 1860 she was swamped. Everything on deck was swept away, her bulwarks were stove in and the cabins were flooded. To make matters worse she sprang a leak, requiring the crew to pump at the rate of 250 strokes an hour.

Battered and broken and with an exhausted crew she entered the Channel on New Year's Eve although her exact position had still not been determined. It was here that she sighted the brig *Aire,* a vessel in even more distress, being in a "sinking state", according to a later account in *The Star.* The *Aire* was sailing from London to Malta with over 300 tons of much-needed Government stores when she was struck by a heavy sea. One of the crew, Marmaduke Richardson, was swept overboard, along with the ship's binnacle, companion way, skylight and boats. The *Aire* was displaying a reversed Union Jack to denote the vessel was in distress.

When it was realised that a French brig, three miles to the leeward of the *Aire,* was paying no attention to the distress signals, the crew of the crippled *Bostonian* decided to go to her aid. The crew of the *Aire* were pleading to be taken off their sinking vessel but given the conditions – heavy seas and gale force winds – Capt Brookman was concerned about risking the lives of his own exhausted crew. The Chief Officer, Captain W W D F Bowers, described as a man of striking presence, stepped forward and offered to make the rescue attempt in one of the *Bostonian's* quarter boats. He was joined by two other volunteers, John Campbell and Joseph Thompson.

In appalling conditions the trio managed to rescue the *Aire's* crew but just as their boat was being hauled alongside the *Bostonian* a towering wave crashed down. An account in Boston's *Sunday Telegram* recorded: "The boat was stove and the men made a leap for life, all of whom succeeding in grappling the mizzen chains, from which they were drawn to the deck by many willing hands."

But that was merely a foretaste of the drama and tragedy that was still to unfold.

In the belief that they were nearer the English coast than they were, the officers of the Bostonian – no doubt reinforced by Captain Slingsby, Master of the *Aire* – decided to take a south easterly course. It was not long before the cry went up "breakers ahead!" and, in spite of some desperate last minute manoeuvring, the *Bostonian* struck the Hanois rocks with great force. Within minutes the ship settled and sank, only the topmasts standing proud of the foaming water.

57. The memorial at L'Éree, Guernsey, to the 17 men and a young woman, who lost their lives when the Cypriot cargo vessel Prosperity was wrecked on the island's west coast in January, 1974. The Mission to Seamen Society raised a fund to erect the memorial. (Author)

Twenty four men then began a fight for survival. Most of them managed to cling to the masts and rigging. Capt Brookman tried to fetch a life buoy but he was swept away and drowned. Chief Mate Bowers swam for a piece of wreckage; as he grasped it a spike went through his wrist. Yet in spite of this painful wound he still managed to reach the safety of a mast.

It was not long before the cold and exhaustion took their toll. One by one, members of both crews, succumbed and dropped in to the water to drown. Some of the others cut pieces from a sail still above the water and took turns to beat each other to keep their blood circulating.

At daylight the three masts – and the remaining pitiful crew – were sighted by Rocquaine pilots and fishermen who immediately put out in their large gig for the rescue. These "hardy toilers of the deep" managed to pluck the sailors to safety and they were brought ashore to be fed, clothed and housed by the "hospitable residents" of Pleinmont.

In total, 18 men had been rescued; 13 from the *Bostonian* and five from the *Aire*. Six men had lost their lives in addition to Marmaduke Richardson who had previously been swept from the *Aire*. Those who died were Capt Brookman and three of the crew from the *Bostonian* and the mate and a sailor from the *Aire*.

There was also considerable loss of property, with an estimated value totalling at least £70,000, a considerable sum in the 1860s. The value of the *Bostonian* was put at £10,000 while her cargo was valued at between £25,000 and £30,000. The British troops stationed in Malta were also inconvenienced for the *Aire* was carrying new clothing, as well as powder, shot and other ammunition.

Capt Bowers, the Chief Officer of the *Bostonian* was later presented with a telescope by the British Government in recognition of his bravery in rescuing the crew of the Aire.

The 13 pilots and fishermen who rescued the crews from the Hanois rocks were not forgotten either. In a letter dated January 29th, 1861, Major General Marcus John Slade, the Lieutenant Governor of Guernsey praised the "promptitude and skill" displayed in the rescue. And he lists the names of those heroes – names that still resonate in the island today:

Frederick Palot
Abraham Le Lacheur
John Le Sauvage
Hellier Le Lacheur
Jean Corbin
Abraham Gallienne
Elie Robilliard
Nicholas Brouard
Nicholas Robilliard
Jean Sarre
Pierre Sarre
Abraham Corbin
Jean De La Mare

A few weeks later the Government, through the Board of Trade, ordered that the sum of five pounds should be distributed to the rescuers as a testimonial to their bravery.

The seafaring descendants of some of those honoured men featured in another notable Hanois rescue about 60 years later. This time is was thick fog that enticed the steamer *Grandest* to her peril. The ship, owned by M Hauser and Sons of Cardiff, was carrying a cargo of anthracite coal from Swansea to Guernsey when she encountered dense fog off the Hanois reef early on the morning of Saturday, November 20th 1920.

Although the ship was motoring at half speed with everyone on watch she struck the reef just a quarter of a mile from Les Hanois lighthouse. The Master, Captain M E Humphries of Caernarvon, said later he had neither seen nor heard any warning signals.

The badly damaged vessel drifted, sinking rapidly. Capt Humphries ordered his crew of 10 to abandon ship, just in time for within 45 minutes from striking the rock the vessel went down some two miles north east of the lighthouse.

Two warning rockets were sent up from the lighthouse and the fishermen of Rocquaine quickly responded. Mr G S Le Couteur decided to take out both of his motor boats, *Le Souvenir* and *L'Esperance*. Joining him in *Souvenir* were Edmund De La Mare, William De La Mare and Nicholas Le Sauvage, while Jean De La Mare's sons and Walter Fallaize took *L'Esperance*. They set off at 6.45 am, just 75 minutes after the *Grandest* had first struck the reef.

Within 15 minutes the two boats were at Les Hanois lighthouse where the keeper, a Mr Morris told them that an unknown steamship had struck the rocks and had drifted – in a distressed state – in a north easterly direction. The rescue party followed in pursuit.

According to the *Gazette* the "courageous rescuers" spotted a flag floating in the water and shortly afterwards three rowboats came into view. Two of these boats contained the captain and all of his crew while the third was that of Jean De La Mare who had come across the shipwrecked sailors while tending his lobster pots. All three boats were taken in tow and the flotilla returned to shore, landing safely below Fort Grey at about 8.30 am.

In spite of their harrowing experience the crew were unharmed. Once ashore they changed into dry clothing before boarding a bus provided by a Mr Sarre. They were then all driven to St Peter Port – the Master; the Second Officer, Isaac Hackett of Arklow; the Third Officer, John Williams of

Port Madoc; and the other members of the crew, Michael O'Brien, Pat Hackett, Joseph Ivory, J Murray, Manuel Domingues, P Crowley, J Irving and T Rees.

Tragically, the Master and crew of the Liverpool sailing ship *Powerful* had been less fortunate when they struck the Hanois reef, in a gale in the winter of 1865. The ship, built in Quebec, Canada, was bound from Calcutta to London with a cargo comprising 50 tons of sugar, 1,320 hundredweight of ginger, 1,250 bales of jute, 140 bags of shellac, 6,000 hides, 25 tons of oilseed and 900 cases of castor oil.

On board were the master, his wife and a child, and a crew of about 30. *The Star* of January 19th, 1865, reported: "There can remain no doubt that this vessel has been lost off this island – probably not far from the Hanois lighthouse – and, as to be feared, with all hands."

The sea, off the west coast of Guernsey, was strewn with wreckage for a month after the disaster. The figurehead of the vessel – a seven feet high kilted Highlander – was washed ashore on the island of Lihou while other items recovered included sail yards, a seaman's chest, part of a carpenter's tool chest, part of the ship's wheel, a caulking box, a barometer, and four wooden fenders. More poignantly, some children's toys, a pocket book and a Bible were also recovered.

Contraband was among the goods recovered from the cutter *Pitt* that was wrecked with heavy loss of life – 11 women and one man – in Perelle Bay in November 1819. The vessel was bound from Jersey to Falmouth in Cornwall with 15 passengers and a cargo of cattle when she was driven on to rocks in strong winds.

When the bodies of the drowned women were later recovered they were found to be wrapped in valuable silks hidden under their everyday clothes. The women, who were probably wives of soldiers garrisoned in Jersey, had been smuggling. Guernsey's Royal Court gave permission for the unclaimed property found on the corpses to be auctioned.

Down through history Guernsey pilots have demonstrated their courage – as well as their intimate knowledge of the dangerous coastal waters – time and time again but on one notable occasion they were involved in their very own mishap some two and a half miles from Les Hanois... much to their embarrassment. The incident happened on April 13th, 1910 when conditions were relatively benign by Guernsey standards.

The island's Pilotage Committee had chartered the steamer *Alert* so that three officers of the London and South Western Railway Company could take their pilotage examinations. Clearly, the committee were intent on making a day of it for a number of guests were invited along for the cruise as well.

The maritime talent on board was impressive. For in addition to Captain Sebire of the *Alert* there were Captains Jones, Mahy, Brouard, Bichard and Lenfesty of the committee as well as the three LSWR officers, Messrs Noyon, Legg and Sarre. In spite of (or, maybe, because of) this wealth of knowledge and experience, the vessel struck Boue Sarre rock, near Lihou, north east of Hanois. No serious damage was done, other than dented pride. Perhaps surprisingly, all three candidates passed their test. "Pity they didn't pass the rock", commented the magazine *John Bull* a few weeks later.

In concluding this history of Les Hanois lighthouse and, by association, the exploits of Guernsey's sea-faring community, it is perhaps ironic that we should end on one of the most recent and photogenic of incidents. On January 3rd 2003 the brand new freighter *Vermontborg* was driven

58. The bulk carrier Elwood Mead that was driven on to Les Grunes de Nord-Ouest rocks, north west of Guernsey, at Christmas 1973. This was the ship that Les Hanois keeper Robbie Goldsmith had reported being aground with "all its lights on", only to be teased for having too much Christmas tipple. (Guernsey Press)

aground on La Capelle reef, less than three miles from Les Hanois, and neither the warning beacon of the lighthouse nor the skills of the pilots could have prevented the accident. For the vessel was without engines and unmanned.

The 120-metre ship was being towed from the Black Sea to Holland – where she was to be fitted out – when her tow lines broke in a force 10 gale west of Les Hanois lighthouse. The vessel drifted helplessly until she was stranded, eventually to become high and dry, on La Capelle. Security staff and salvage teams kept vigil at what became a notable tourist attraction. Holes in her hull were patched up while the Dutch salvage specialists waited for a suitably high tide. Then on January 18th two tugboats, *Anglian Prince* and *Boxer,* towed the vessel free from the rocks, around Guernsey's coastline and on to Harlingen in the Netherlands.

While observing the huge hull, worth £1.5 million, perched on the rocks, readers of *Guernsey Globe* had fun speculating on what the stranded vessel might be used for, if salvage operations proved unsuccessful. "Turn it into a Guernsey version of the Tate Modern Gallery" was one suggestion. Another idea was that the hull should be used as a new debating chamber for Guernsey's legislature – "there would be plenty of volunteers to man the tow ropes and set them adrift so that we could all enjoy the peace and quiet". But perhaps the most appropriate suggestion came from a reader who thought the soundproofed hull should be used as a nightclub for older people, called "The Old Wrecks' Club".

SHIPWRECKS ON AND AROUND THE HANOIS ROCKS, GUERNSEY

Date	Name	Type of Vessel	Location	Fate (where known)
Pre 1309	?		Perelle Bay	
1663 - Feb 17	?	Fishing boat	St Saviour's	
1734 - Dec	?		Lihou	
1767 - Jan 2	Exchange	540 tons	Houmet	Wrecked; 6 men lost
1771 - Oct 11	Henrietta	Foreign vessel	Hanois	
1776 - Jan 22	"Galiot"	Dutch Galiot	Pleinmont	Wrecked; all lost
1777 - Dec	Sprightly	Naval cutter	SE of Hanois	Capsized and sank
1807 - Nov 28	Boreas	Naval frigate	Hanois	Sank; 127 men lost
1816	?		Off West coast of Guernsey	
1816 - Nov 11	Marie Elizabeth	Danish Dogre	Rocquaine Bay	
1816 - Dec 6	Sampson		Lihou	
1816 - Dec 13	St Alexy		Off West coast of Guernsey	
1817 - Feb 14	?		Rocquaine Bay	Wrecked; all lost
1817 - June 1	?		Off West coast of Guernsey	
1819 - Nov 26	Rose	Sloop	L'Éree	Wrecked; 13 lost
1819 - Nov 26	Pitt	Cutter	Perelle Bay	Wrecked; 11 lost
1820 - Jan 12	La Rose Victoire		Hanois	
1820 - May 12	?	Chasse Marée	Rocquaine Bay	Abandoned and towed in
1821 - Dec 10	Pere de Famille		L'Éree / Perelle Bay	Wrecked; all lost
1824 - Sep 30	L'Ursule Cherie	Chasse Marée	Fort Richmond	
1828 - Jan	Mary	Cutter	Corbin Rock, Rocquaine	Wrecked; hull sold
1828 - May 23	Jeanne Marie Joseph	Chasse Marée	Lihou then Rocque au Nord	Struck Lihou; wrecked on Rocque au Nord
1831 - Apr 30	La Marie Francoise	Cutter	Portelet	
1834 - Nov 6	Buccleugh	Schooner	Sambule/Grunes	Lost on Hanois
1835 - Dec 30	George William		Hanois	
1835 - Dec 30	Vrou Catharina	Galiot	Crocq Bay	Wrecked; all lost
1836	?	Galiot	Hanois	
1836 - Jan 29	Alfred Anne	Brig	L'Éree	Went aground; 2 lost

Date	Name	Type of Vessel	Location	Fate (where known)
1836 - Mar 28	Thomas M Lyon	Brig	Off North West Guernsey	Sank
1838 - Feb	?		Off West coast of Guernsey	Wrecked; all lost
1838 - Feb	?		Off West coast of Guernsey	Wrecked; all lost
1840 - May 27	Vertueux	Chasse Marée	Rocquaine Bay	
1840 - June	Esperance		Off West coast of Guernsey	
1840 - Sept 16	?	Chasse Marée	Rocquaine Bay	Foundered; all lost
1841 - Jan	?		Off West coast of Guernsey	
1843 - Jan 1	Susan	Schooner	Off West coast Guernsey	Drove ashore Vazon; salved
1843 - Feb 3	Rob Roy	Pilot cutter	Off West coast of Guernsey	Towed in to Rocquaine
1846 - Oct 7	Union	Schooner (100 tons)	Lihou	Salved; towed to Brest
1848 - Mar 3	Five Sisters	Brig	Perelle Bay	Wrecked; 5 bodies washed up
1849 - Jan 1	Napoleon	Brig	West Guernsey	Towed in; crew rescued
1849 - Apr 27	Robert Bradford	Barque	Rocquaine Bay	Dismasted and towed in
1849 - Nov 16	Europe	Barque	Fort Houmet	Wrecked; all but one lost
1849 - Dec 17	Sainte Anne	Chasse Marée	Fort Pezeries	Salved
1849 - Dec 19	Oneida	Packet Ship	Perelle Bay	All saved; wreck sold
1850 - Feb 7	Victoria	Brig	Rocquaine Bay	Towed in
1850 - Oct 2	Infanta		WNW of Guernsey	Foundered
1851 - Nov 20	Le Locman	Brig	NW coast	Taken to Portelet where became wreck
1852 - Jan 24	?	Chasse Marée	Hanois	Crew presumed lost
1852 - May 27	George and Elizabeth	Cutter	Rocquaine Bay	Beached Portelet; salved
1852 - Aug 4	Marie Rose	Chasse Marée	Rocquaine Bay	Towed in
1853 - Apr 4	Trois Susannes	Cutter	Rocquaine Bay	3 lost; hull sold
1853 - Dec 24	Reindeer	Schooner-brig	Sambule	Wrecked; 3 lost
1854 - Apr 28	L'Adele	Brig	Lihou	Wrecked; 2 lost
1857 - Jan 11	Jeune Marie	Schooner	Lihou	Towed in
1858 - Feb 21	Alliance	Schooner	Black Rock, Rocquaine Bay	Salved
1858 - June 1	Concordia	Schooner	Rocquaine Bay	Salved
1858 - Sept 16	Arcana		Hanois	Salved

Date	Name	Type of Vessel	Location	Fate (where known)
1858 - Nov 30	?	Ketch	Sambule	
1860 - Jan 21	Constant	Schooner-galliot	Rocquaine Bay	
1860 - Mar 24	Endymion	Barque	L'Éree	Went aground
1860 - Nov 5	Les Deux Amis	Chasse Marée	Off Hanois	Towed in
1861 - Jan 1	Excelsior	Cutter	Hanois	Capsized; crew reached Sark
1861 - Jan 3	Bostonian	Cargo vessel	Hanois	Sank; all rescued
1862 - Apr 6	Globe	Schooner	Struck Hanois or Lihou	Foundered off L'Ancresse
1865 - Jan 15	Powerful	Cargo vessel	Off West coast of Guernsey	Sank; all lost
1865 - Mar 7	Frederick William		Black Rock, Rocquaine Bay	Salved
1866 - Feb 14	?		Off West coast of Guernsey	Wreckage washed up at Pleinmont
1867 - May 2	Silvia		Rocquaine Bay	Wreckage washed up on Lihou
1869 - May 27	Branch		Hanois	Wrecked; crew saved
1869 - Aug 14	?		Hanois	
1871 - Sept 16	Nord	Steamship	Sambule	
1871 - Oct 21	Lucie		Off West coast of Guernsey	Wreckage washed up on Lihou
1881 - Dec 24	Dugald Stewart		Picked up off Hanois	Struck at Amphrocques
1882 - Mar 22	Laura Ann	Schooner	Hanois	Salved
1883 - Sep 4/5	Entreprenant	Cutter	Pendu	
1883 - Nov 17	Arrow	Cutter	Off NW coast of Guernsey	Went aground
1886 - Aug 30	Belfort	Steamer	La Pendule/ La Selle	Wreck sold
1887 - Oct 30	St Lukas	3-Master	Pezeries	One drowned/ wreck sold
1888 - Apr 13	Yorouba	Brigantine-rigged steamer	Off Lihou	Sank
1890 - Apr 7	Auguste and Louise	Brigantine	Between Les Tielles & Pleinmont	
1891 - Apr 25	Collina		West coast of Guernsey	
1891 - Dec 8	Nord		NW of Fort Richmond	
1892 - Mar 29	Vigoureaux	Mackerel boat	Hanois	Drifted ashore dismasted
1892 - Nov 17	Ida (formerly Abbey Town)	Barque	Perelle Bay	Went aground

Date	Name	Type of Vessel	Location	Fate (where known)
1892 - Dec 12	Esperance		Off West coast of Guernsey	Damaged boat washed ashore
1894 - Nov 14	?	Sailing vessel	Lihou	
1894 - Dec 14	?		Off West coast of Guernsey	
1896 - Dec 20	Buzulzo	Steamship	Rocquaine Bay	Sank; 2 seamen washed Ashore
1897	?		Pendu	
1899 - Aug 28	Alert	Steamship	Perron Rock; beached in Rocquaine Bay	Repaired
1901 - Aug 26	Courier	Steamship	Grande Etacre	Salved
1903 - Sep 22	Anne	Schooner	Black Rock, Rocquaine Bay	Salved
1904	Roman	Steamship	Hanois	
1905 - Jul 27	Trignac	Steamship	Soufleuresse	Made St Peter Port under own steam
1910 - Apr 13	Alert	Steamship	Boue Sarre, near Lihou	Reached harbour
1910 - Mar 24	Gem	Barquentine	Black Rock, Rocquaine Bay	Salved
1911 (or 1912)	Mauve	Steamship	Hanois	
1912	?		Hanois	Wrecked
1913 - May 6	Emily Warbrick	Schooner	Off Hanois; (in collision with Jewel)	Reached harbour
1913 - May 6	Jewel		Off Hanois	Reached harbour
1914 - Jan 4	Busy Bee	Schooner	Black Rock, Rocquaine Bay	Salved
1914 - Feb 11	Vedanta	Sailing barge	Braye Rock, Roccquaine Bay	
1915 - Apr 30	Trio	Steamship	Hanois	Towed in
1917 - May 27	Mary Anne	Brigantine	West Guernsey	Towed in
1920 - Nov 20	Grandest	Steamship	Hanois	Sank; crew rescued
1921 - Sep 14/15	Louise Gustave	Schooner	Off West coast of Guernsey	Burned offshore
1924 - June 24	Dunvegan	Steamship	NW Hanois	Reached harbour
1929 - June 3	Glencreagh	Steamship	Perelle Bay	Salved
1930 - Oct 23	Arguenon	Ketch	Black Rock, Roccquaine Bay	Salved
1932 - Jul 10	Drayouz L'Ehcet	Fishing boat	Lihou	Salved
1932 - Sep 22	Capri	Yacht	Pezeries Point	Sank under tow

Date	Name	Type of Vessel	Location	Fate (where known)
1933 - Mar	Evasion	Yacht	Hanois	Foundered
1963 - Feb 5	Johann Collett	Trawler	Off West coast of Guernsey	Foundered; nine saved
1965 - May 28	La Salle	Motor cargo vessel	Soufleuresse	Sank; crew of 40 rescued
1972 - Oct 18	Causette	Fishing vessel	Hanois	Sank under tow
1974 - Jan 16	Prosperity	Motor cargo vessel	La Conchée Rock, off Perelle Bay	Went aground, broke away and sank
2003 - Jan 3	Vertmontborg	Container ship (new and under tow)	La Capelle reef after losing tow West of Hanois	Went aground, refloated and salved

Source:

J M David - The Early History of the Hanois; Transactions of Société Guernesiaise, Vol XV11, 1961 p 224.

E W Sharp - Transactions of Société Guernesiaise, 1967.

Guernsey Museums & Galleries

"Guernsey Wrecks; Shipwrecks around Guernsey, Alderney and Sark" by the author.

LIGHTHOUSE KEEPERS AT HANOIS*

SERVED FROM	SERVED TO	NAME	RANK
1865	1867	Roberts –	AK
1873		Freeman – G	AK
1882		Cutting – TG	AK
1892		Odden – HT	AK
1893		Warden – WH	AK
1893		Jarvis – JH	AK
1897		Sunaway – HE	AK
1898		Batton – WJ	PK
1899		McCarthy – RH	AK
1901		Clague – W	AK
1902		Lloyd – WH	AK
1902		Temple – TA	PK
1906		Frost – A	PK
1908		Horne – E	AK
Post 1909		Brereton – HA	AK
1910		Kaye – WJ	AK
1945	1949	Trezise – Cyril	PK
1945	1946	Gallienner – TV	AK
1946	1951	Robert – Freddie	PK
1946	1946	Mahy (or Maky) – HW	AK
1947	1948	Martel – PO	AK
1947		Jaeger – LE	AK
1948	1949	Allen – HH	AK
1949	1950	Woodruff – HD	PK
1949	1949	Ewens – RD	AK
1949	1951	Harvey – D	AK
195?		Simon – RJ	AK
195?		Taylor – Harold	AK
195?		McCarthy – John	PK
195?		Curnow – H	AK
1950		Cuthbertson – Tommy	PK
1951		Reynolds – Simon	AK
1951	1955	Whiston – Tom	AK
1951	1953	Pine – Les	AK
1951	1952	Rounds (or Rovids) – D	AK

SERVED FROM	SERVED TO	NAME	RANK
1952	1953	Whitmarsh – HL	AK
1953	1953	Ross – C	AK
1953		Haywood – Charlie	AK
1953	1954	Duff – RJ	AK
1954	1955	Dobinson –	AK
1955		McCarthy – JJ	AK
1955		Packer – Dick	AK
1957		Haywood – Charlie	AK
196?		Jeffers – Richard (Dick)	AK
196?		Kett – Bob	AK
196?		Clarke – KWH	AK
196?		Griffiths – Phil	AK
196?		Humphreys – LW	AK
196?		Pine – Les	PK
196?		Brown – Gordon	AK
1962	1963	Sythes – Desmond (Des)	AK
1969	1971	Cox – John	AK
197?		Spurgeon – Dave	AK
197?		Martinez – Tony	AK
197?		Coyte – RDH	AK
197?		Scott – Bill	AK
197?	1981	Brown – Gordon	PK
197?		Thompson – Bob	AK
1970	1974	Kett – Bob	AK
1971		Quigley – Brendan	AK
1971		Hardy – Mike	AK
1971		Haywood – Charlie	PK
1971		Griffiths – Phil	AK
1971		Douglas-Sherwood – Gerry	SAK
1973		Rowley – Ken	PK
1974	1975	Daniels – Jack	AK
1973	1974	Goldsmith – Robbie	AK
1973	1974	Humphries – Ralph	AK
1973	1978	Wakley – Norman	PK
1974	1975	Taylor – Harold	PK
1974		Briddle –	AK

SERVED FROM	SERVED TO	NAME	RANK
1974		Gill –	AK
1974		Long – Wally	PK
1974	1976	Smith – Pete	AK
1974		Wilkinson – Bob	AK
1975	1977	Williams – Mervyn	AK
1976		Triggs – PR	AK
1977	1981	Horner – Brian	AK
1978	1981	Monk – Ken	PK
1978		Murphy – Dave	AK
1978		Tromans – Bert	PK
1978		Street – Eddie	AK
1978		Brierley – Jack	PK
1978		Golding – K	AK
1979	1989	Goldsmith – Robbie	AK
1980	1981	Clayton – Brian	AK
1980	1984	Stafford – Paul	PK
1981	1986	Jesty – Terry	AK
1981	1985	Tromans – Bert	PK
1982	1984	Brierley – Jack	PK
1982	1984	Shipley – Mark	AK
1984	1984	Boulton – Peter	AK
1984	1988	Davis – Paul	AK
1984	1987	Goldsmith – Robbie	AK
1984	1988	Marsh – Tony	PK
1985	1986	Harris – Brian	PK
1986	1987	Phillips – Gordon	PK
1987	1992	Guest – Gordon	AK
1987	1987	Cairnes – Ian	AK
1988	1989	Losse – Jim	K in C
1988		Grindle – Norman	PK
1988	1988	Williams – Mike	AK
1988	1992	Laing – Alan	AK
1989	1989	Hawkins – Barry	AK
Late 1980s early 1990s		Homewood – Tony	AK
1990	1990	Hawkins – Barry	AK

SERVED FROM	SERVED TO	NAME	RANK
1990	1992	Bowden – Laurie	AK
1990	1993	Harry – Clive	AK
1991		Furse – Phil	AK
1991		Grindle – Norman	PK
1992	1995	Bloy – Barry	AK
1992	1995	Nelson – John	AK
1992	1995	Arnold – Nathan	AK
1992	1994	Parsley – Roland	AK
1992	1996	Goldsmith – Robbie	PK
1993	1996	McGovern – Dave	AK
1994	1995	Aish – Avery	AK
1995	1996	Simmons – Barry	AK
1995		Burdis – Brian	PK
1995	1995	Surplice – Tim	AK
1995	1995	Guest – Gordon	AK
1995	1995	Davis – Paul	AK
1995	1996	Appleby – Dave	PK
	1996	Boulton – Peter	AK

Abbreviations:
PK – Principal Keeper
AK – Assisstant Keeper
K in C – Keeper in Charge
SAK – Supernumerary Assistant Keeper

*Unfortunately, in spite of extensive research this list is inevitably incomplete. Most records of the lighthouse and light vessel service appear to have been destroyed in the 1940 bombing of Trinity House. Furthermore, some of the hand-written entries in Trinity House registers are somewhat indistinct.

It should also be noted that a number of those listed above were doing relief or temporary duties at the Hanois. L.E. Jaeger (1947), for instance, was from Trinity House's Lightvessel Service. He later became Master of the Channel Lightvessel.

Sources:

Trinity House Service List, published 1910 – Association of Lighthouse Keepers archive; No T344

Trinity House Seniority Register; MS 30121

Trinity House Station Book listing keepers and crews 1941-1955; MS 30122

Trinity House seniority and relief lists: G.F.Douglas-Sherwood (private records)

"Hanois Hindsight" published LAMP No 30, March 1996 The Lighthouse Society of Great Britain

Various issues of "Flash", periodical of the Trinity House Service

Other researches by the author.

LES HANOIS LIGHTHOUSE – KEY DATES

1807 *HMS Boreas* shipwreck
1816 *Marie Elizabeth* shipwreck
1816 Lieutenant Governor calls for a light
1817 Trinity House dismisses call for a light
1848 Trinity House urges erection of lighthouse
1848 Guernsey Chamber of Commerce opposes light
1849 Guernsey Chamber of Commerce reverses decision and backs light
1849 10-year argument starts over dues
1859 Trinity House decides to proceed with Hanois construction
1860 Foundation stone laid
1862 Hanois light shines for the first time
1865 *Powerful* lost near lighthouse
1920 *Grandest* wrecked
1940 Guernsey occupied by German troops
1945 Guernsey – and lighthouse – liberated
1964 Lighthouse modernised
1974 *Prosperity* wrecked
1979 Helipad installed on top of Hanois tower
1996 Hanois automated – last rock tower to be demanned
1996 Hanois becomes first rock tower to be fitted with photovoltaic panels
1999 New telemetry and communications system installed
2003 Newly-built *Vermontborg* goes aground

ILLUSTRATIONS

BIBLIOGRAPHY

Bougourd, J Le M – Guernsey Dialect Names, with articles by various authors; publisher and date unknown. Priaulx Library, Guernsey

Boyle, Martin - Bishop Rock, one of the Lighthouses of England and Wales series; B & T Publications, 1997

Boyle, Martin - Eddystone, one of the Lighthouses of England and Wales series; B & T Publications, 1997

Boyle, Martin - Lighthouses: Four Countries - One Aim; B & T Publications, 1996

Boyle, Martin - Lighthouses To Light Their Way; B & T Publications, 1996

Boyle, Martin and Ken Trethewey - Needles Point, one of the Lighthouses of England and Wales series; B & T Publications, 1996

Boyle, Martin and Ken Trethewey - Portland Bill, one of the Lighthouses of England and Wales series; B & T Publications, 1996

Chance, James Frederick - The Lighthouse Work of Sir James Chance, Baronet; CD - The Lighthouse Society of Great Britain; 2001

Coates, Richard - The Ancient & Modern Names of the Channel Islands; Paul Watkins; 1991

Cruickshank, Charles - The German Occupation of the Channel Islands, The Official History of the Occupation Years; Guernsey Press Company 1975 (9th Printing March 1999)

Dafter, Ray - Guernsey Wrecks: Shipwrecks Around Guernsey, Alderney and Sark, Matfield Books; 2001

David, J M - The Early History of the Hanois Lighthouse; La Société Guernesiaise Transactions, Vol XV11:51; 1960

Douglas-Sherwood, G F - A Glossary of Lighthouse Service Terminology; The Association of Lighthouse Keepers; 2000

Edwards, G B - The Book of Ebenezer Le Page; Penguin Books; 1982

Hague, Douglas B and Rosemary Christie - Lighthouses: Their Architecture, History and Archaeology; Gomer Press; 1975

Hugo, Victor - The Toilers of the Sea; Alan Sutton Publishing; 1990

Johnson, Derrick - Lighthouses of England and Wales; David and Charles; 1975

Kilshaw, William - The Friendly Lights: The Story of English Lighthouses and Lightships; Guernsey Press.

Majdalany, Fred - The Red Rocks of Eddystone; Longmans; 1959

Major, Alan - The Kentish Lights; S.B.Publications; 2000

Marr, James - Guernsey Bailiwick Harbours And Landing Places c.2000 B.C. to 1987; Toucan Press; 1987

Marr, James - The History of Guernsey, the Bailiwick's Story; the Guernsey Press Company (revised edition); 2001

Nicholson, Christopher - Rock Lighthouses of Great Britain; Patrick Stephens; 1983

Nicholson, Christopher - Rock Lighthouses of Great Britain: The End of an Era?; Whittles Publishing; 1995

Ovenden, John and David Shayer - Shipwrecks of the Channel Islands; Underwater Video Services; 2002

Parsons, Lynn F - Lighthouses; Shire Publications Ltd; 1995

Peters, John - Hanois, the southernmost Light; Flash - Trinity House; December 1993

Sharp, Eric W - Lighthouses of the Channel Islands, Guernsey Historical Monograph No 17; Toucan Press; 1979

Williams, Peter - Beacon on the Rock, The Dramatic History of Lighthouses from 1600 to the present day; Aurum Press; 2001

Williams, Thomas - Life of William Douglass M.Inst.C.E; Printed for private circulation; 1923

Woodman, Richard - Keepers of the Sea; Lavenham: Terence Dalton Ltd and printed by Lavenham Press; 1983

Woodman, Richard and Jane Wilson - The Lighthouses of Trinity House; Thomas Reed Publications; 2002

****

Guernsey Society Quarterly Review, Winter 1966

"Hanois Hindsight" published LAMP No 30, March 1996

Trinity House Seniority Register; MS 30121

Trinity House Service List, published 1910 - Association of Lighthouse Keepers archive; No T344

Trinity House Station Book listing keepers and crews 1941-1955; MS 30122

Website www.YourMemories.co.uk

INDEX

H

I

J

K

L

M

N

O

T

U

V

W

Y

Z